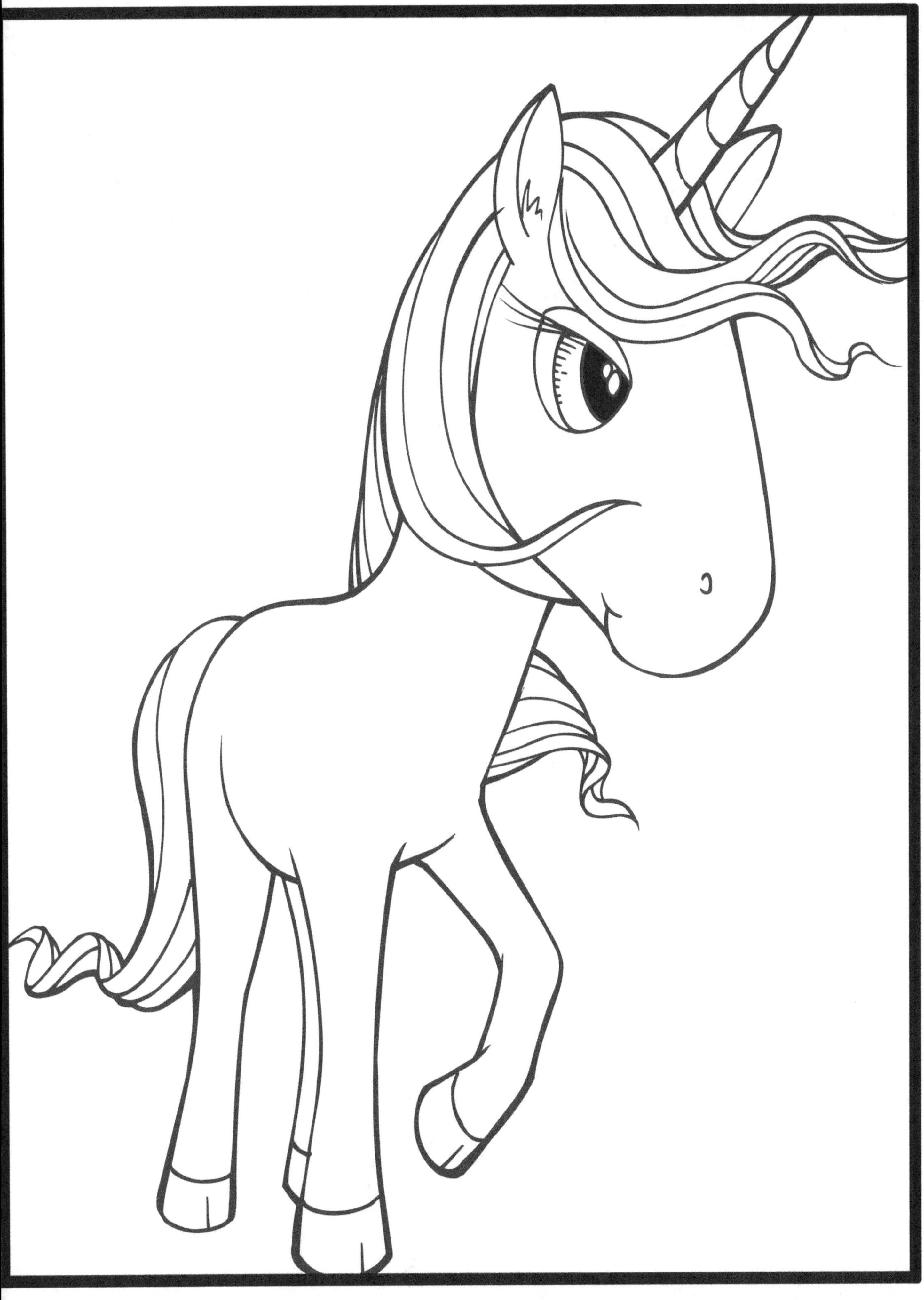

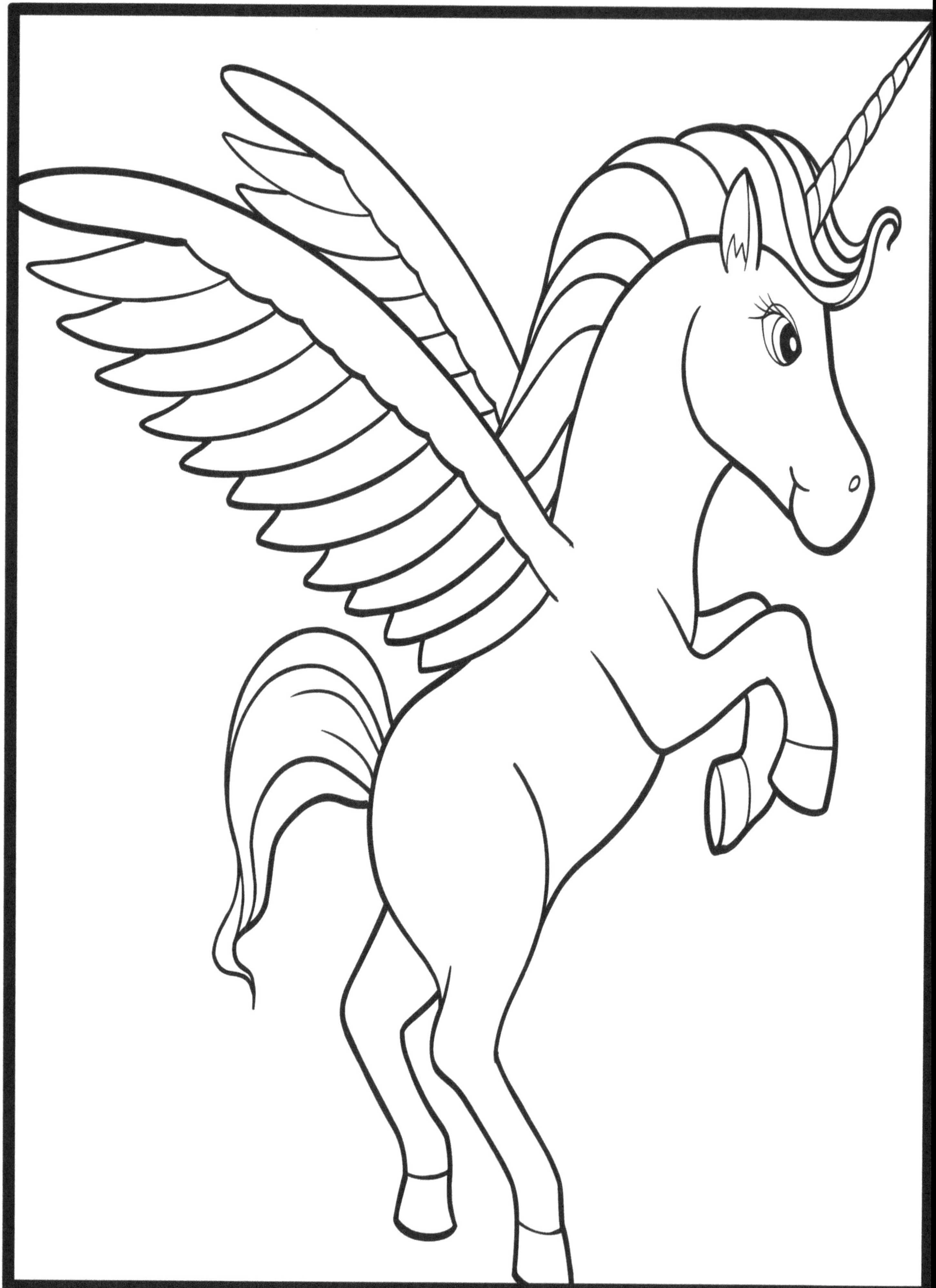

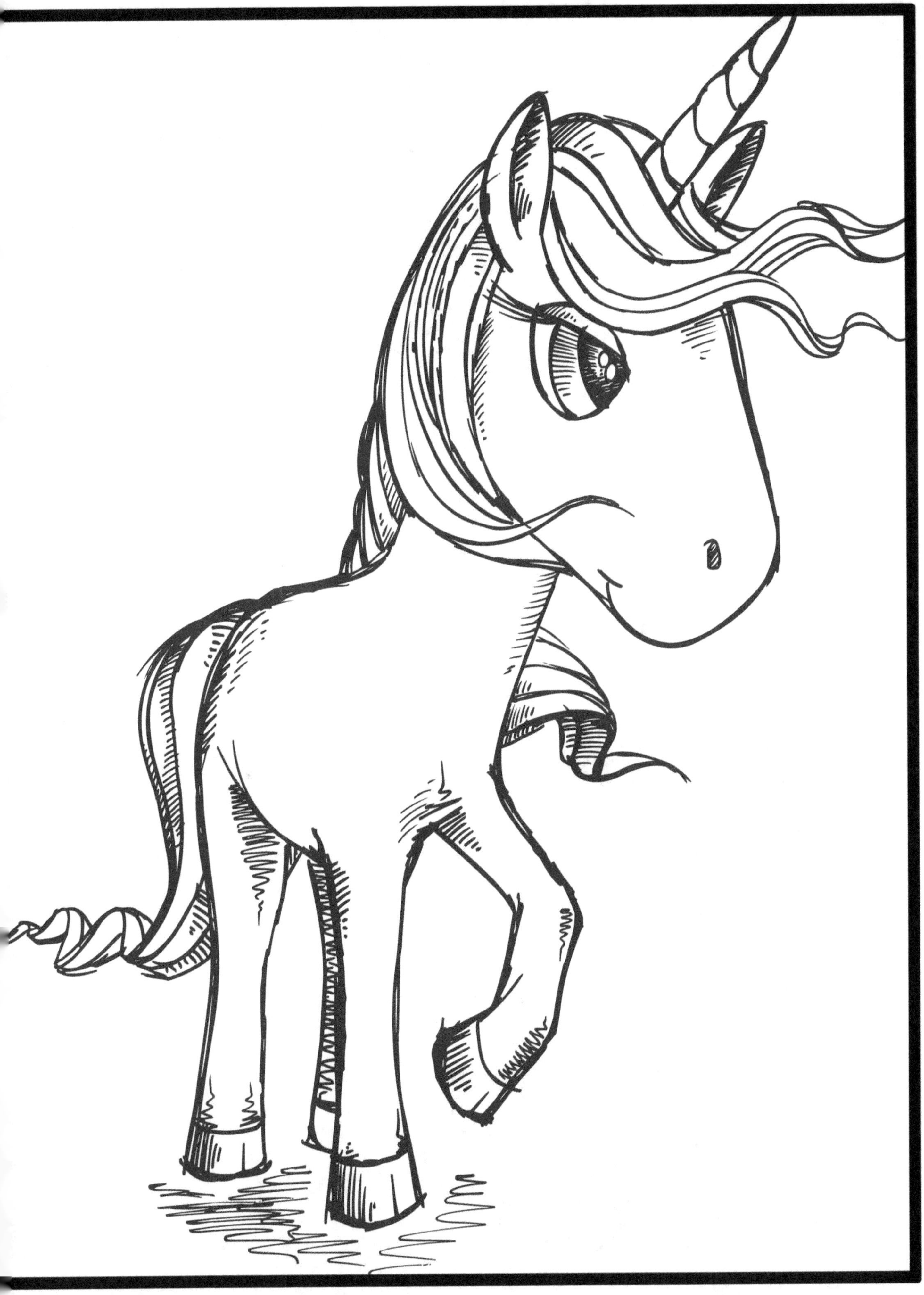

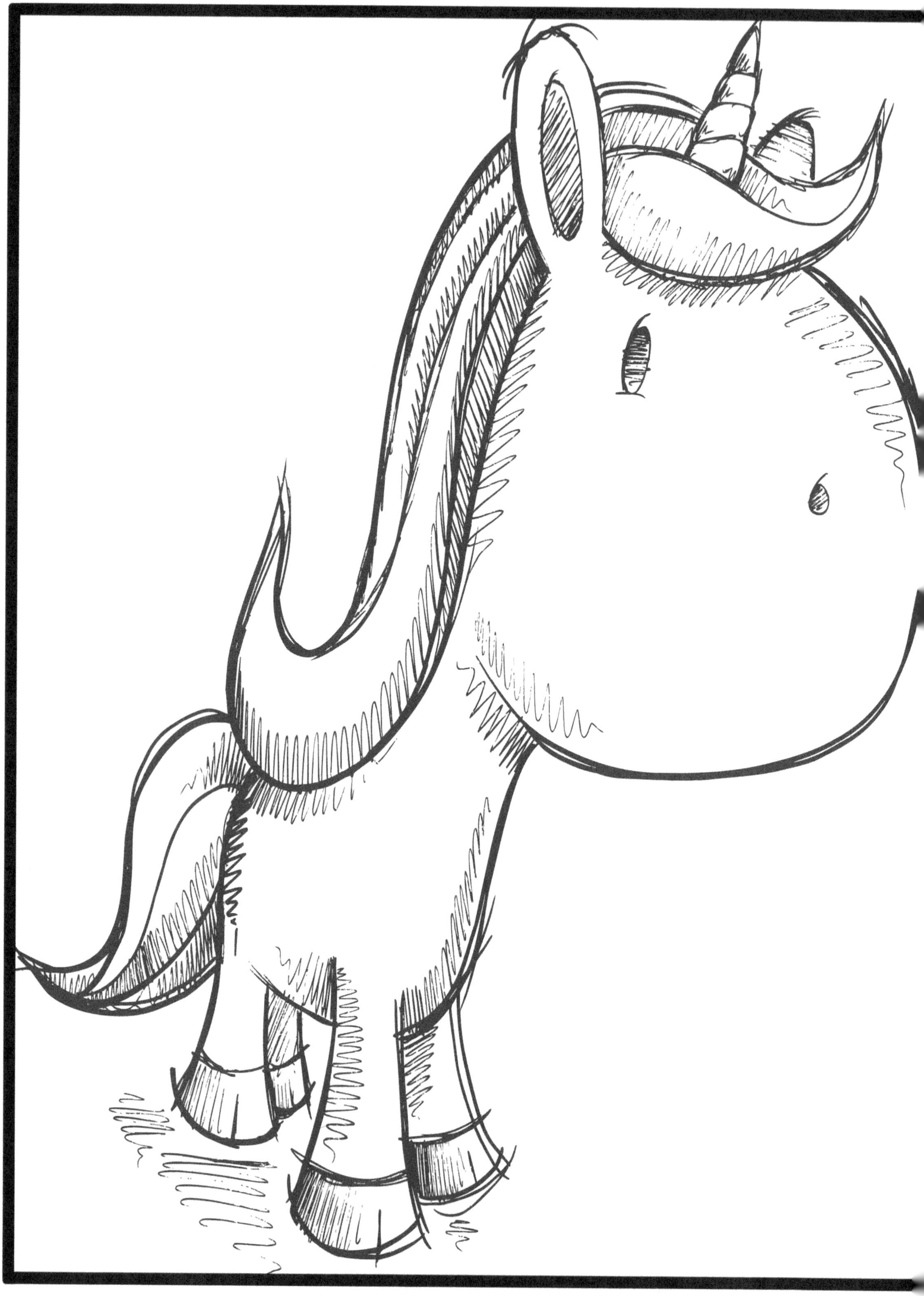

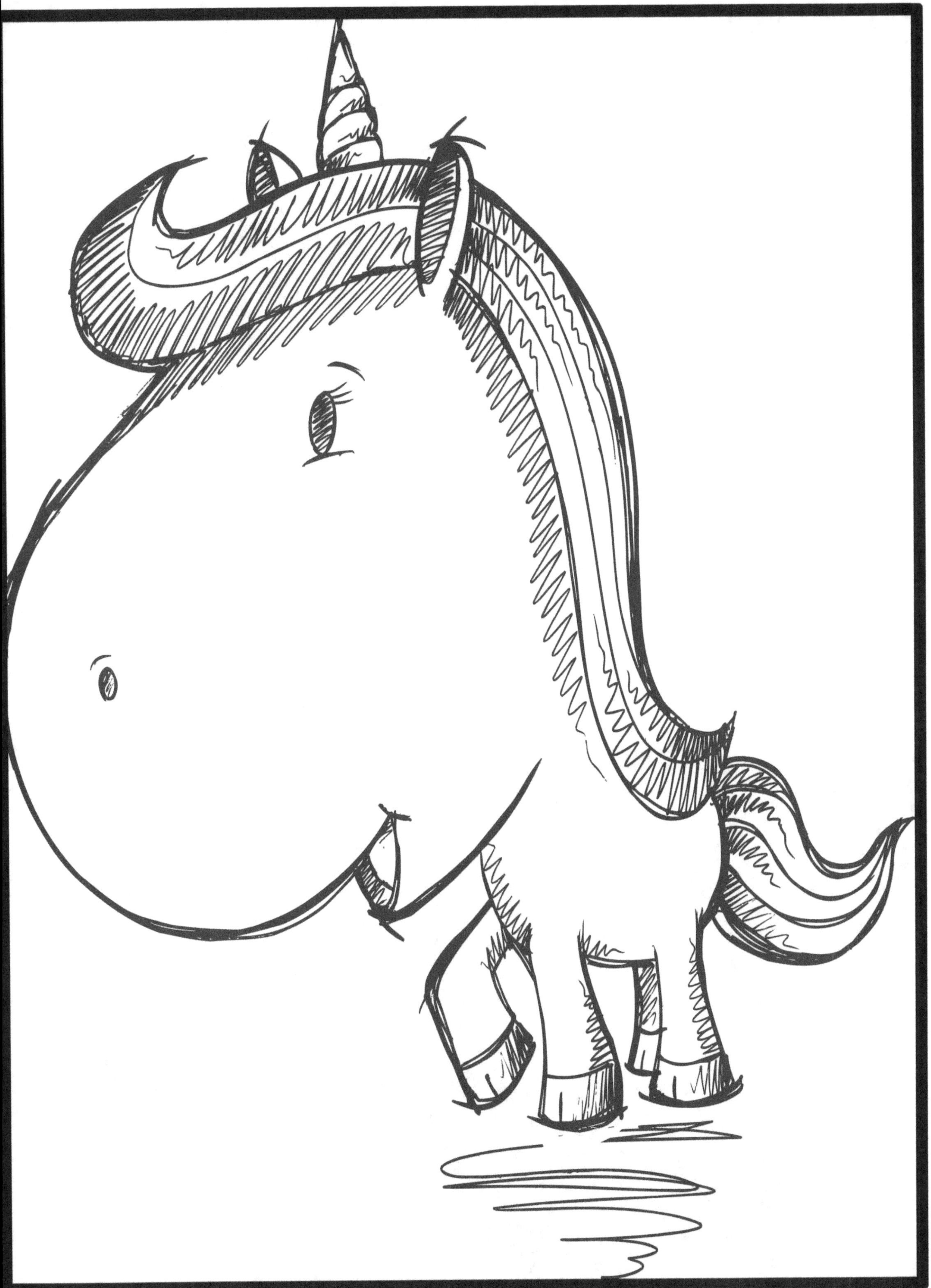

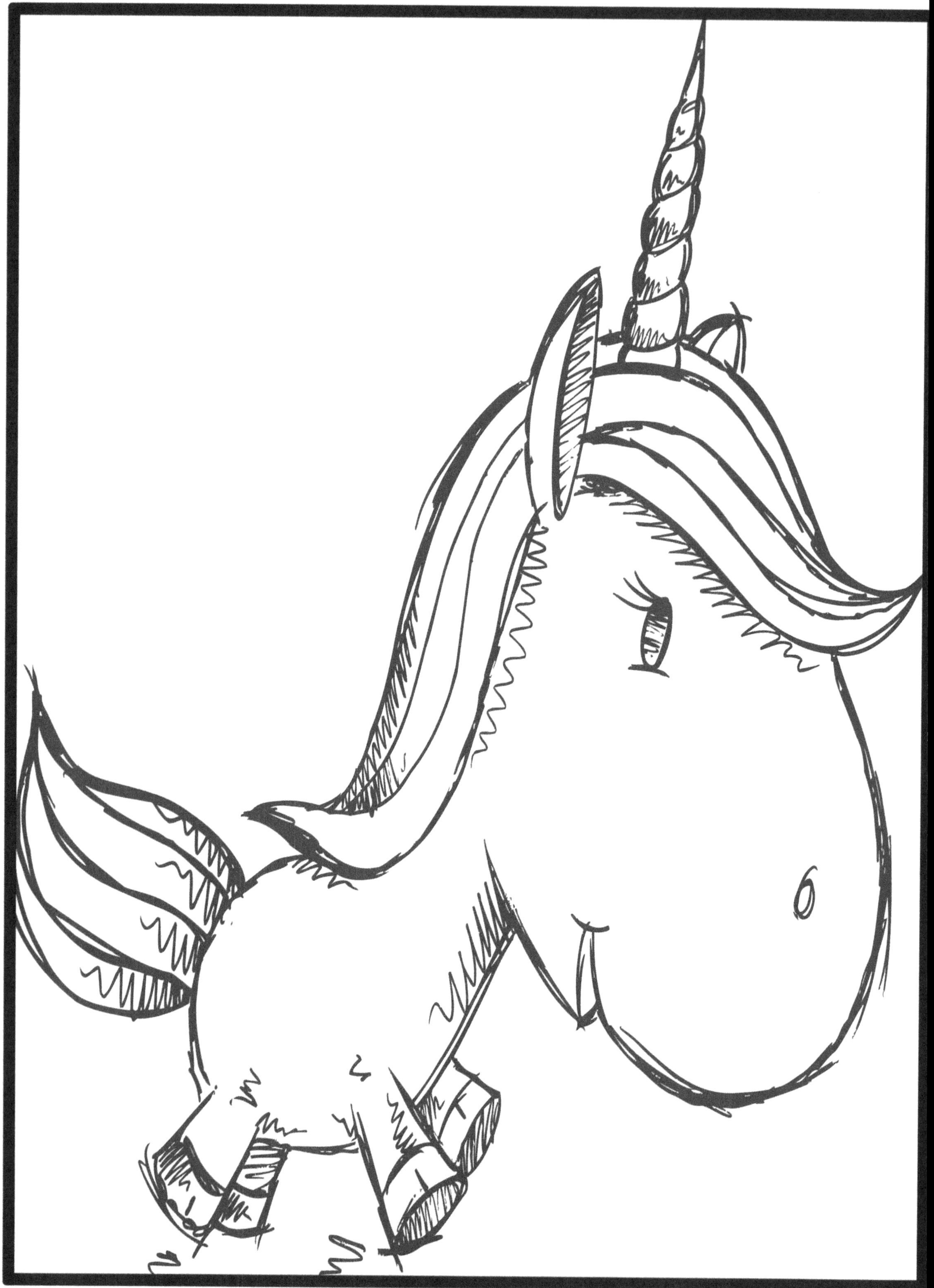

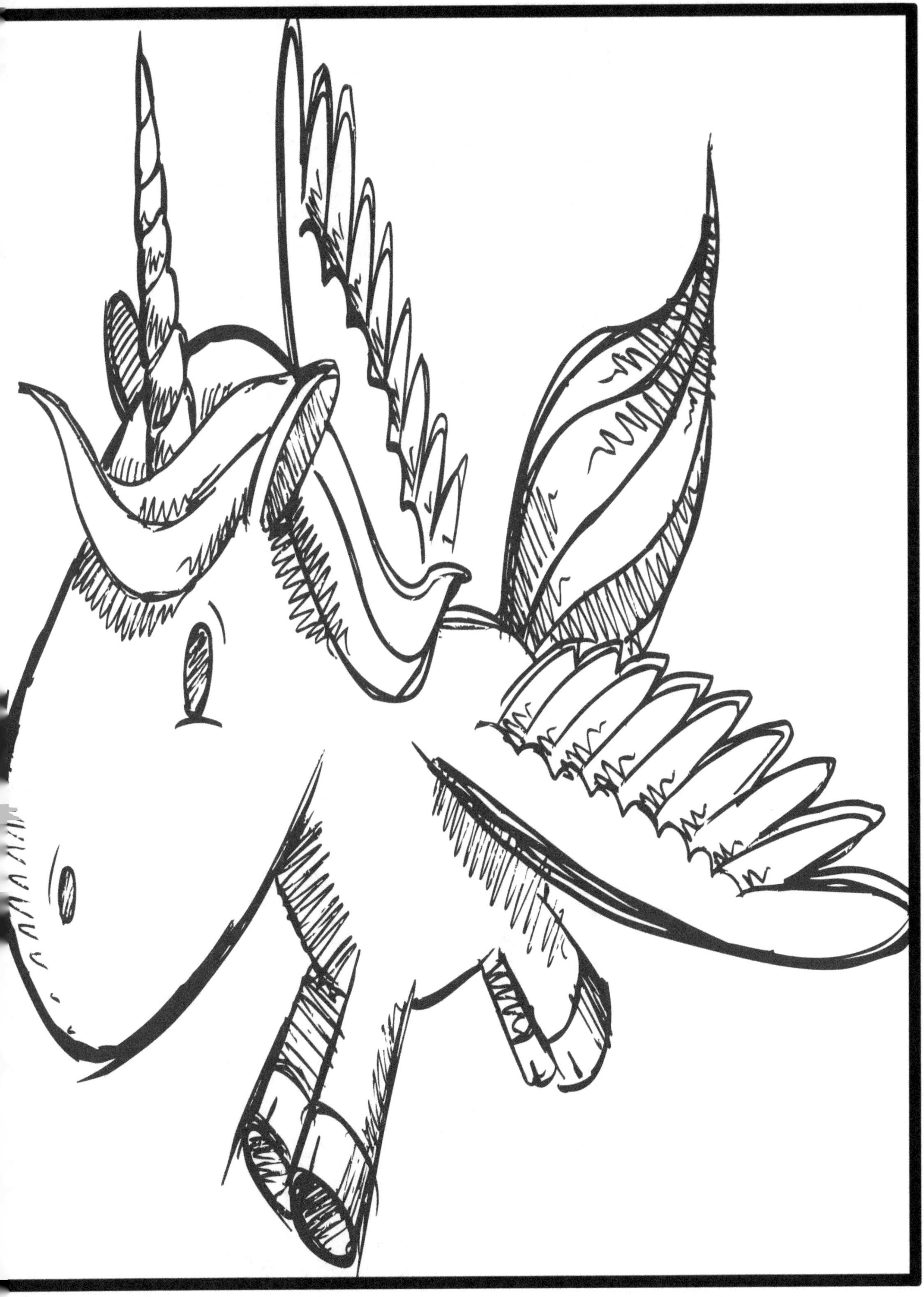

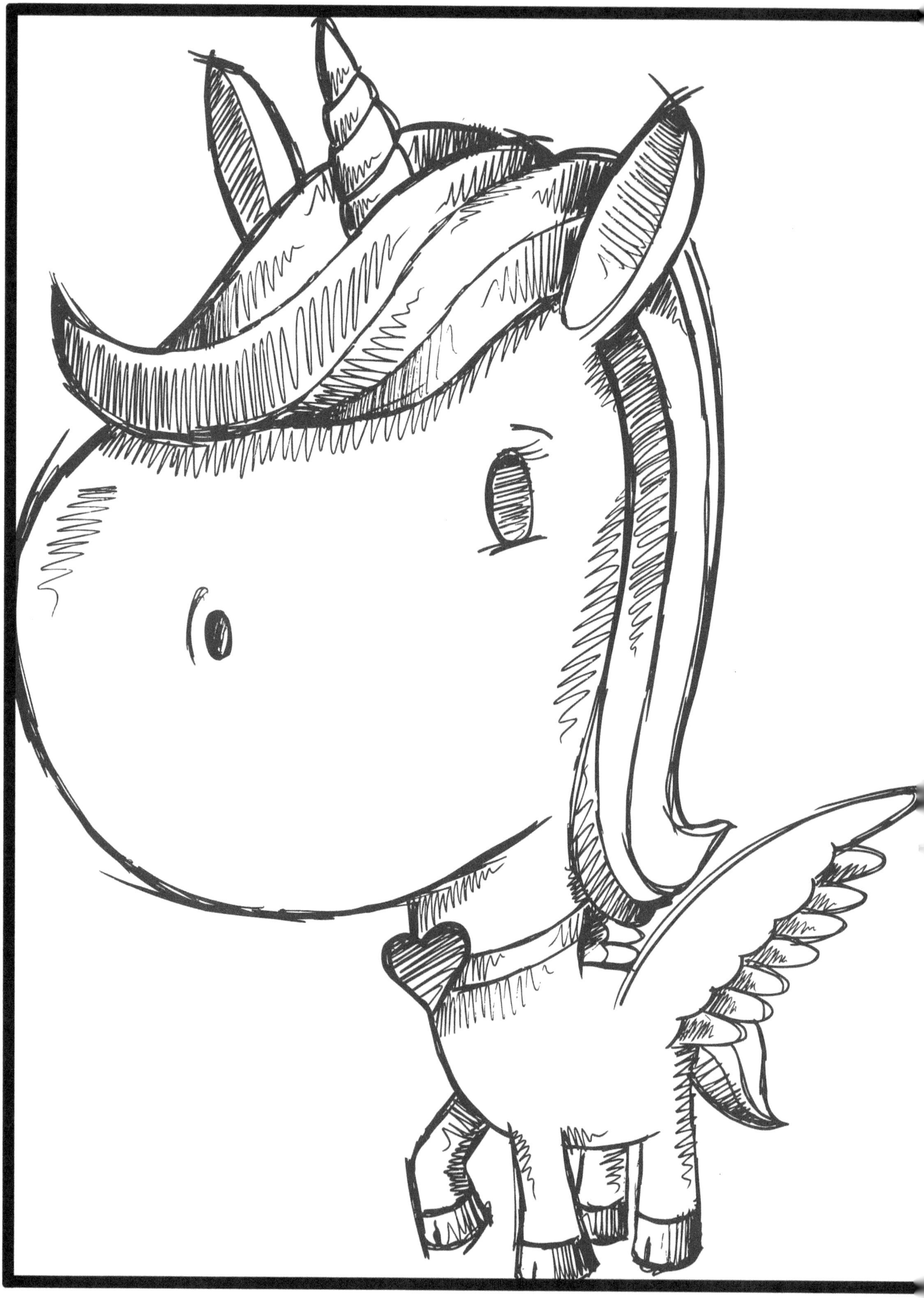

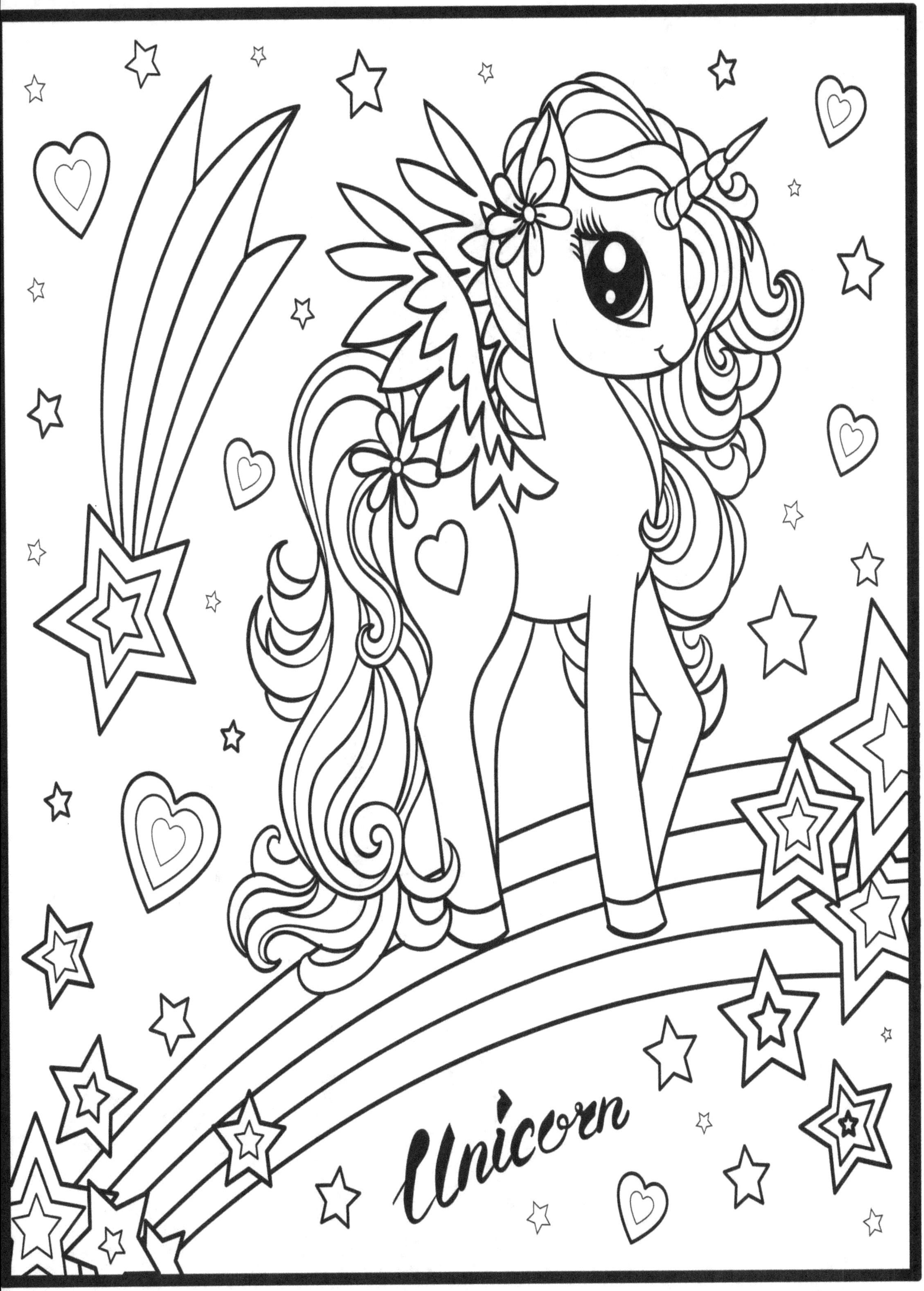
Unicorn

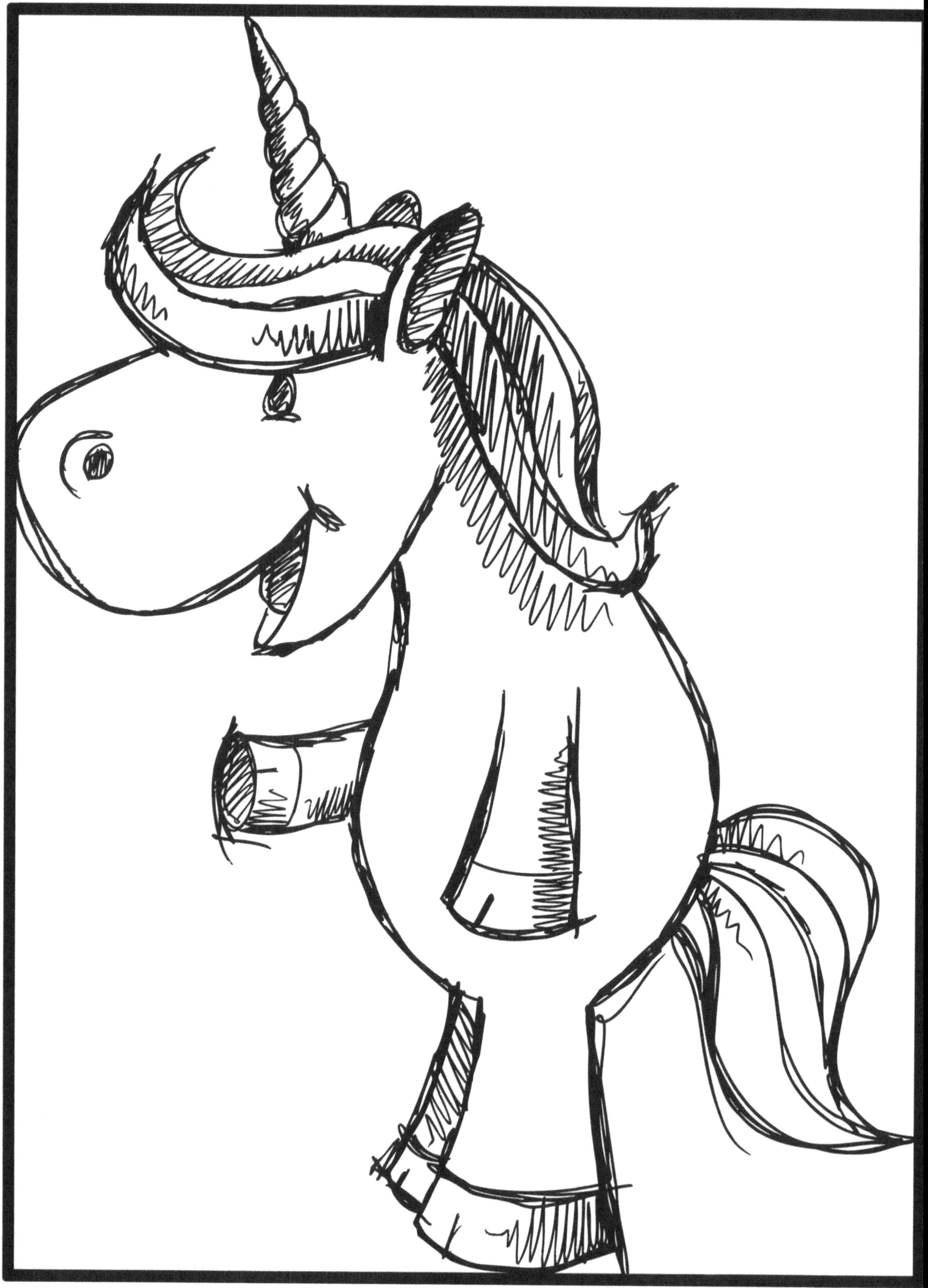

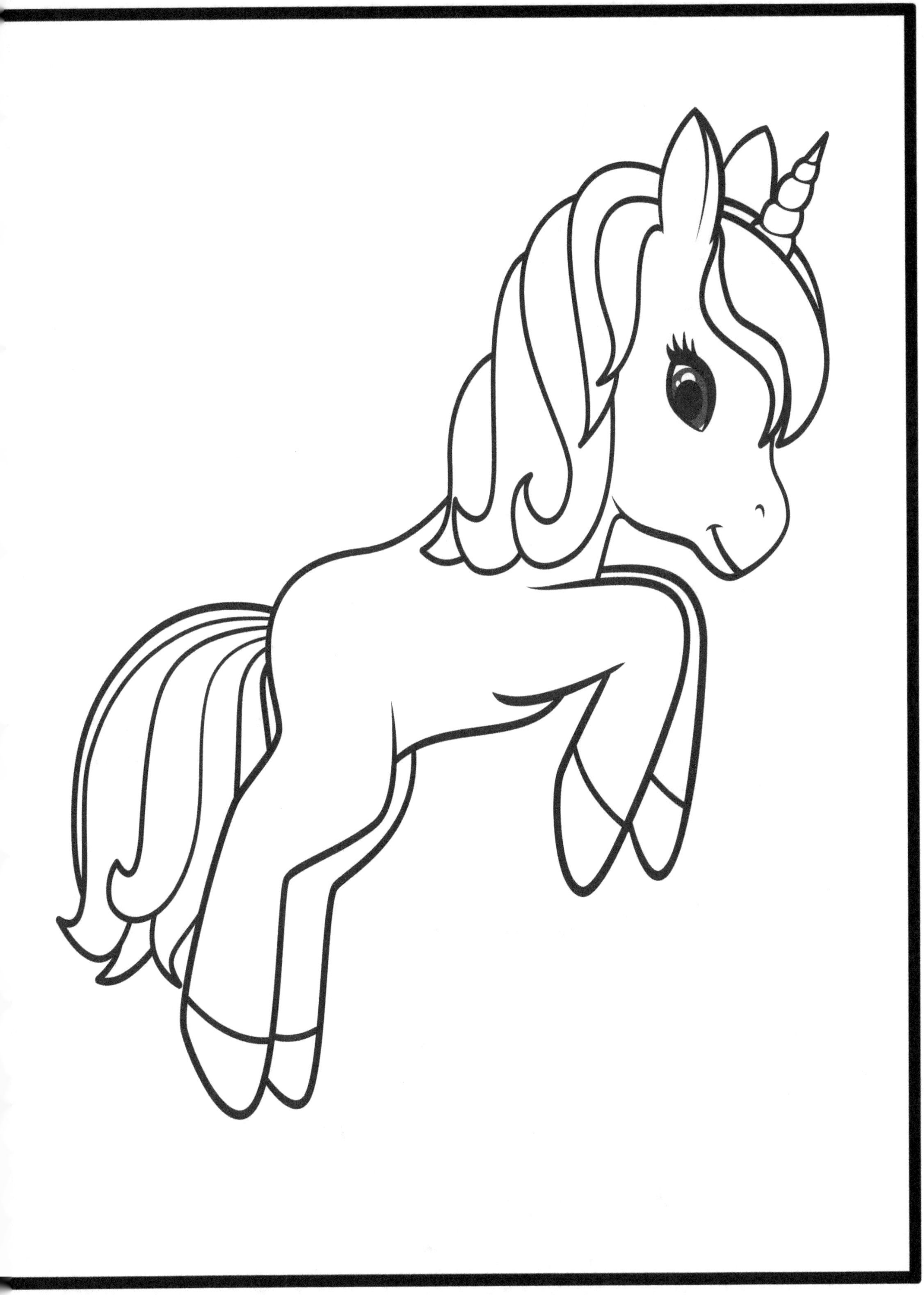

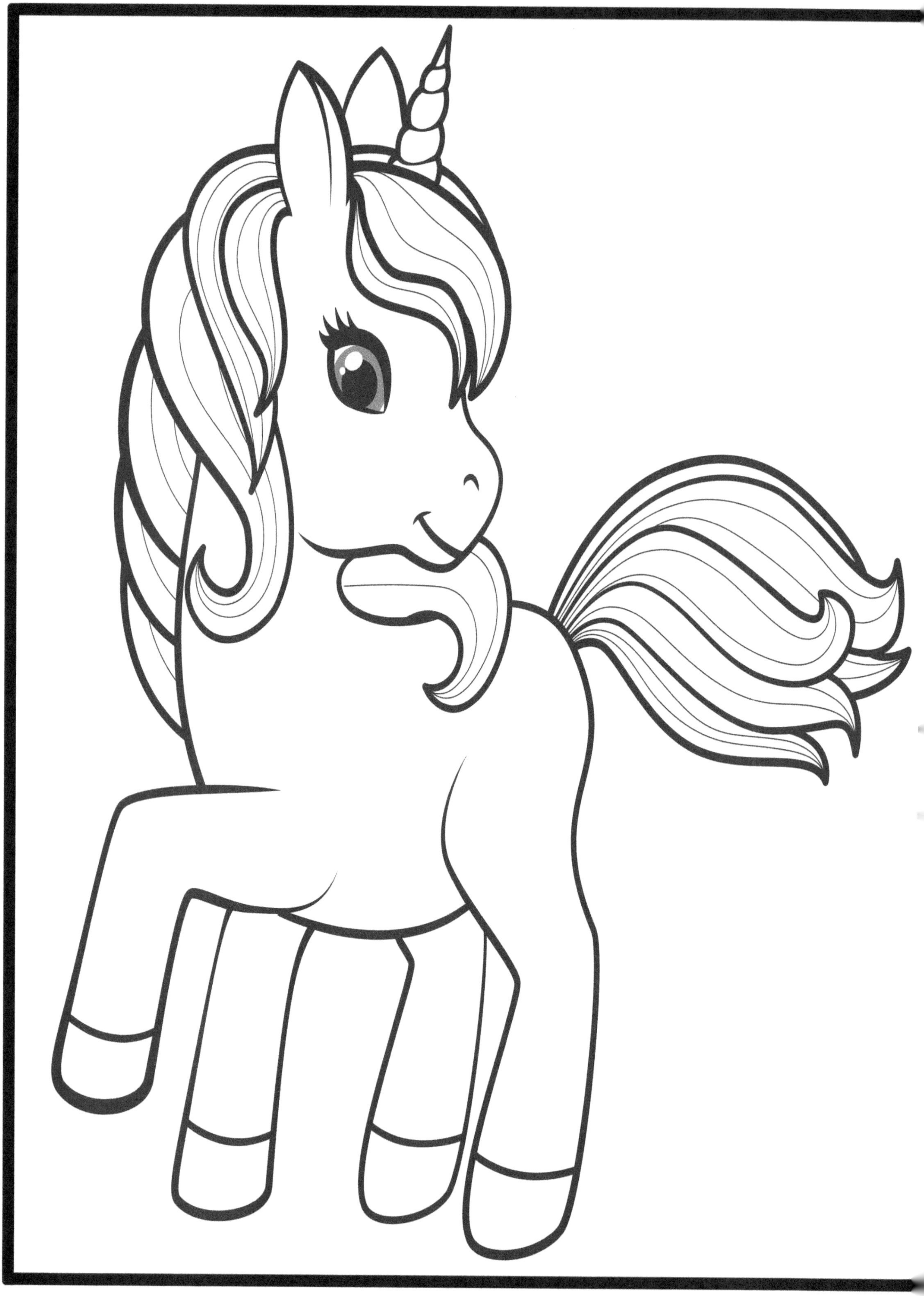

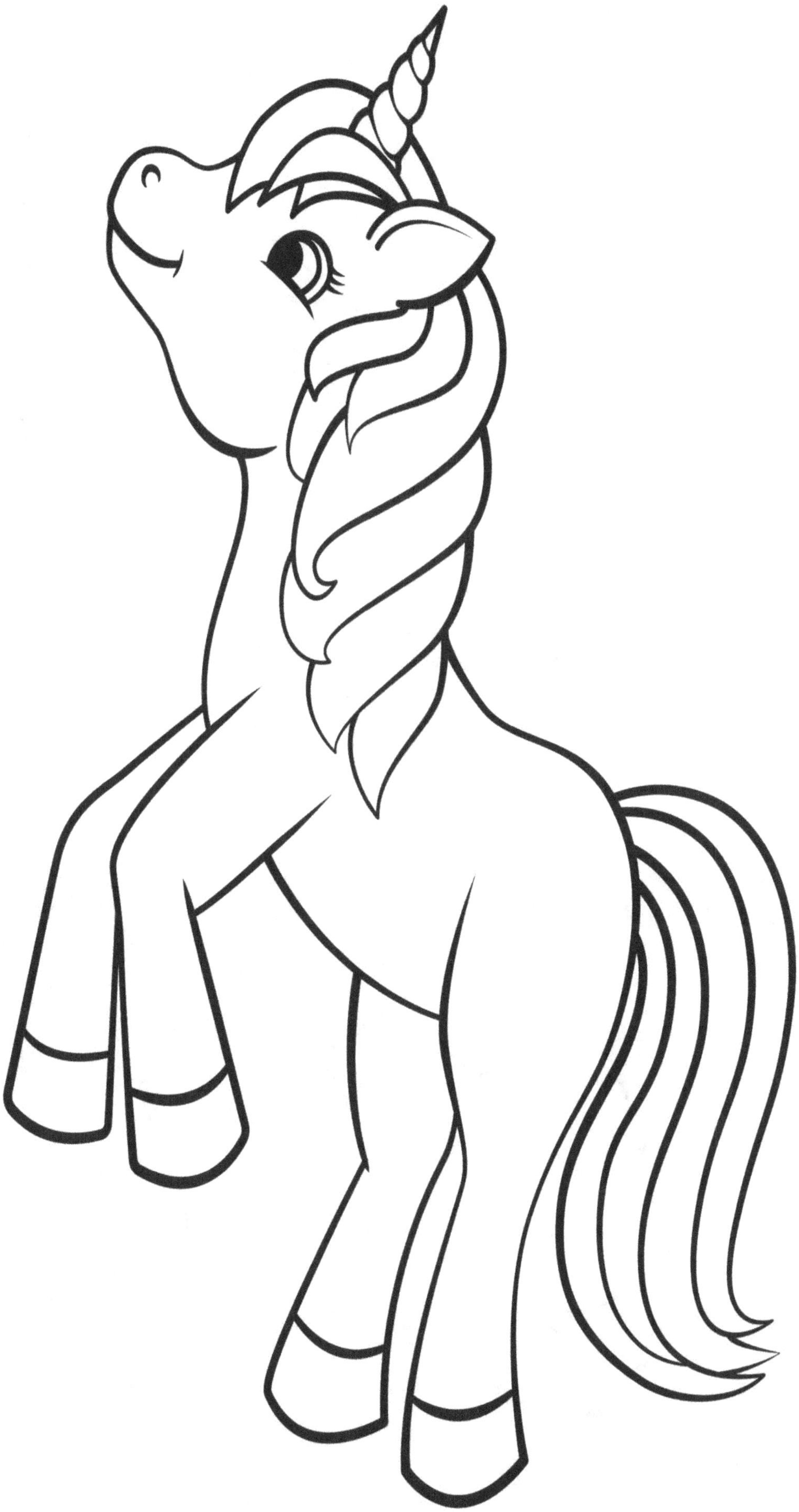

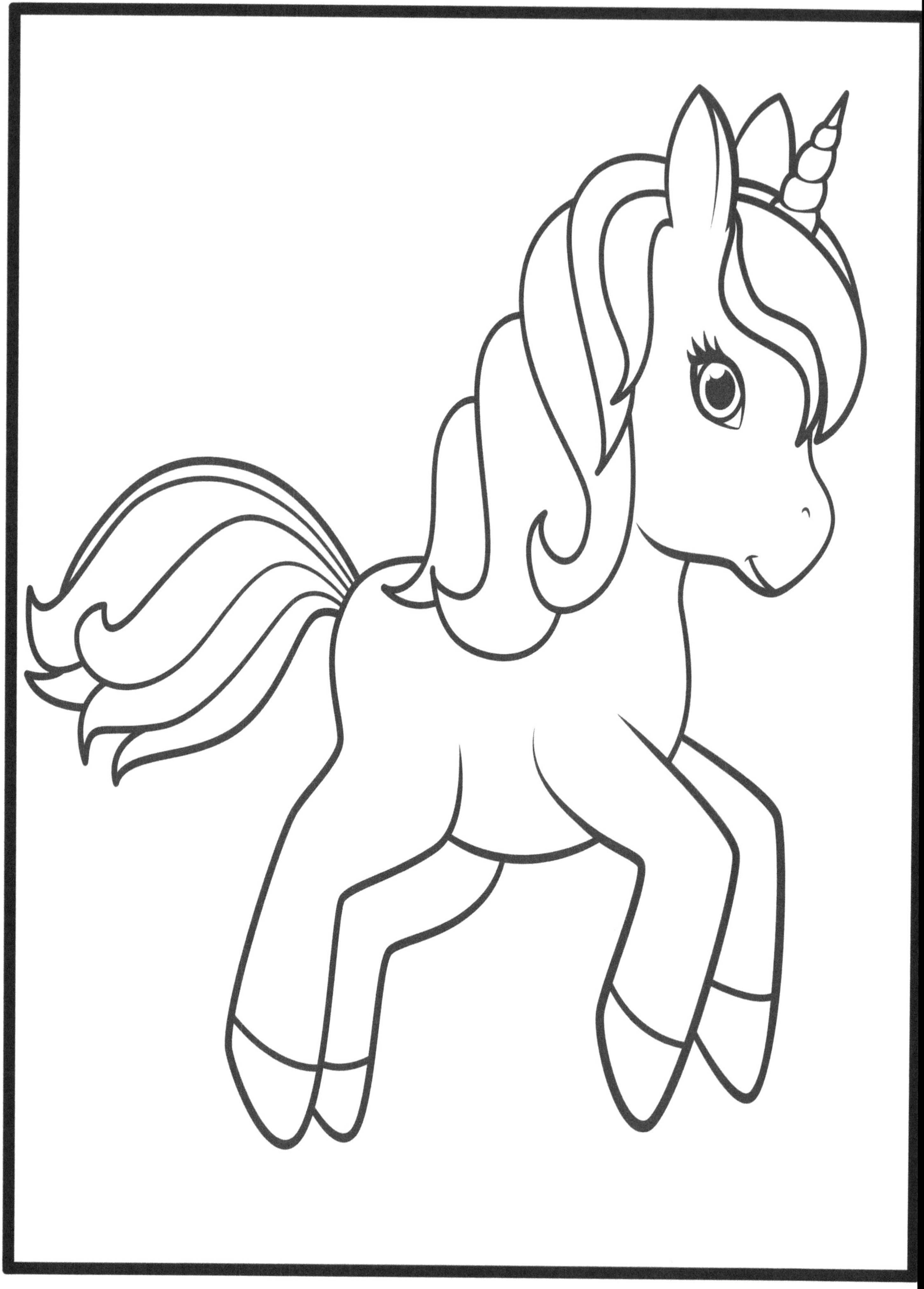

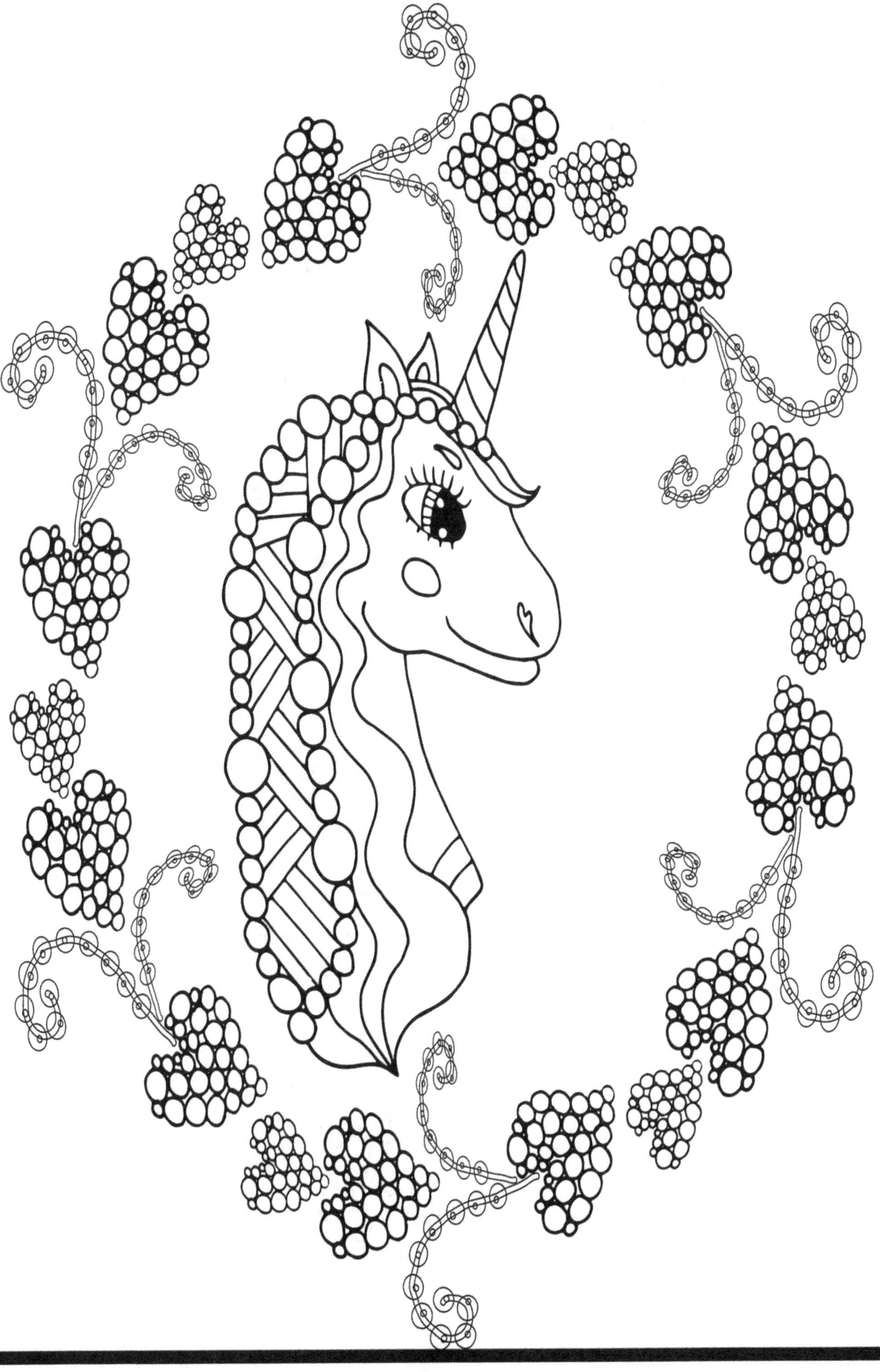

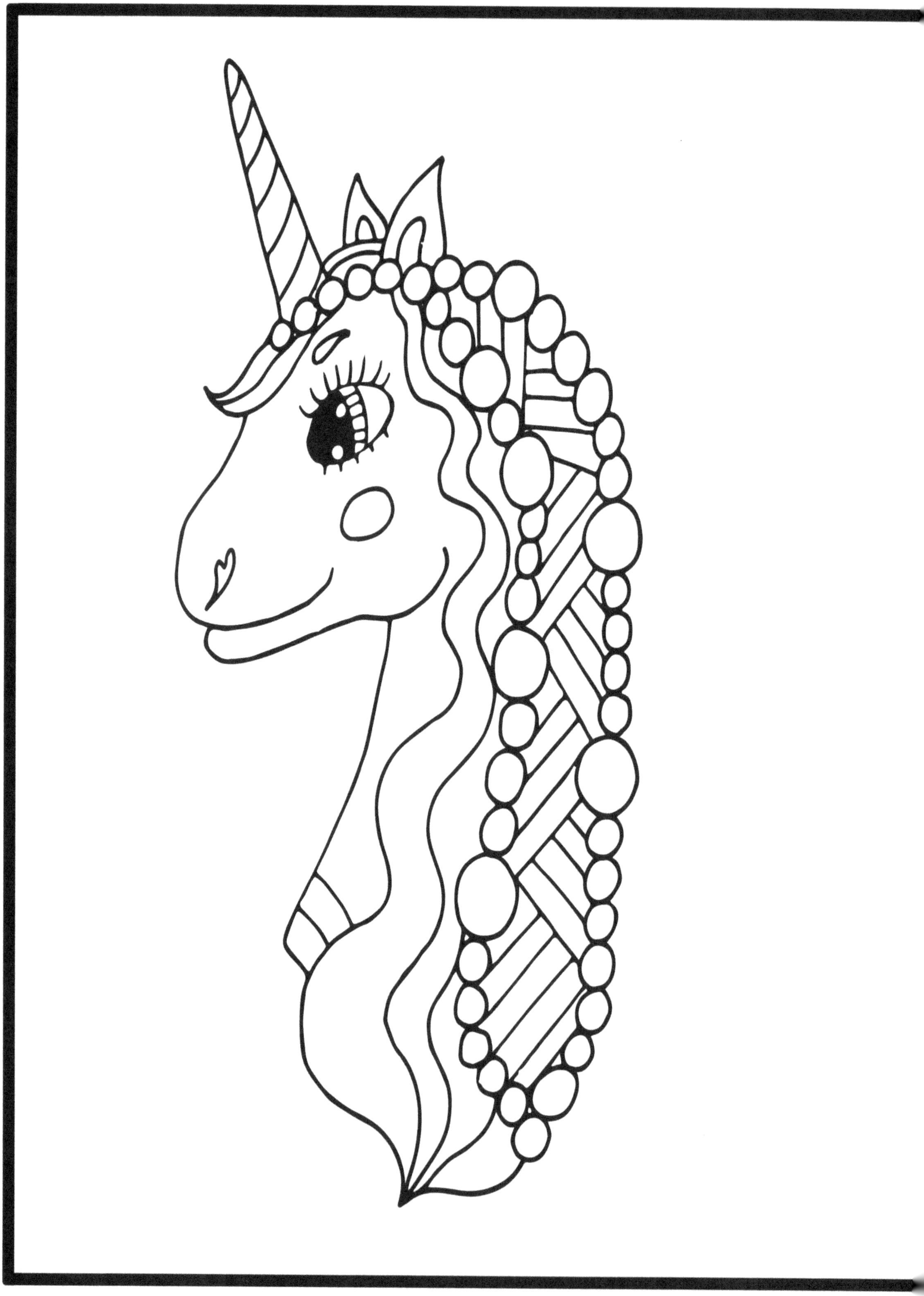

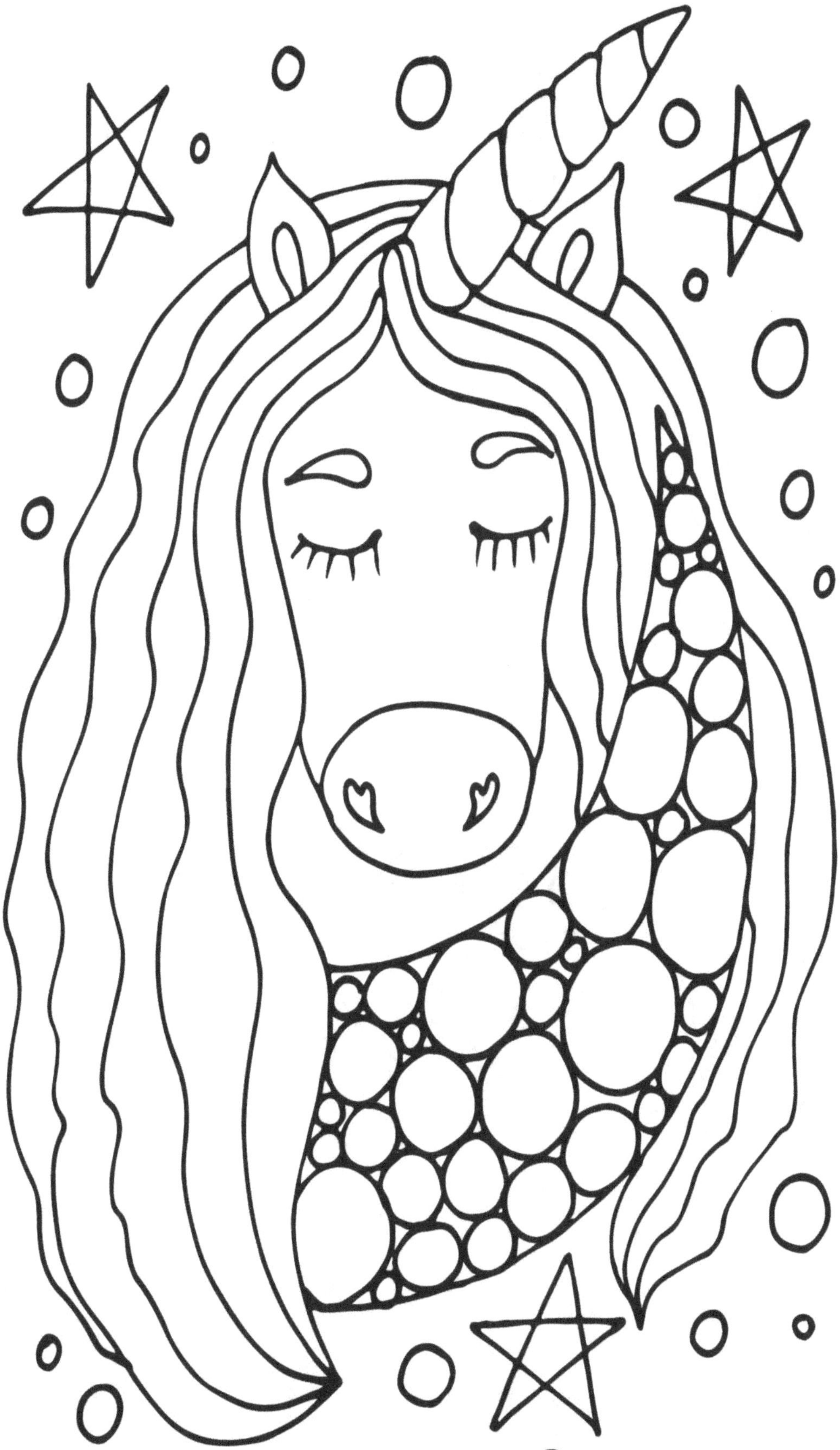

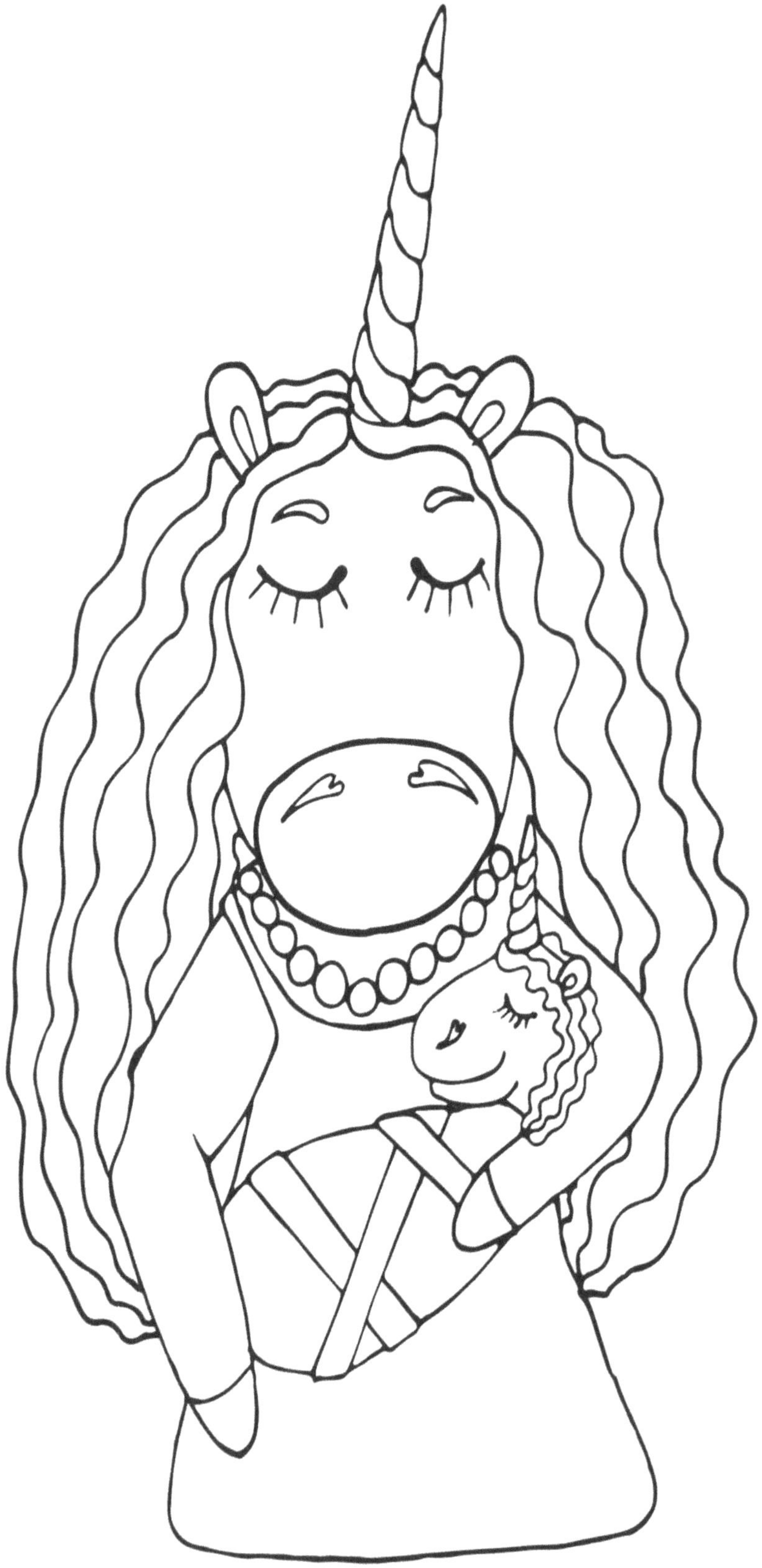

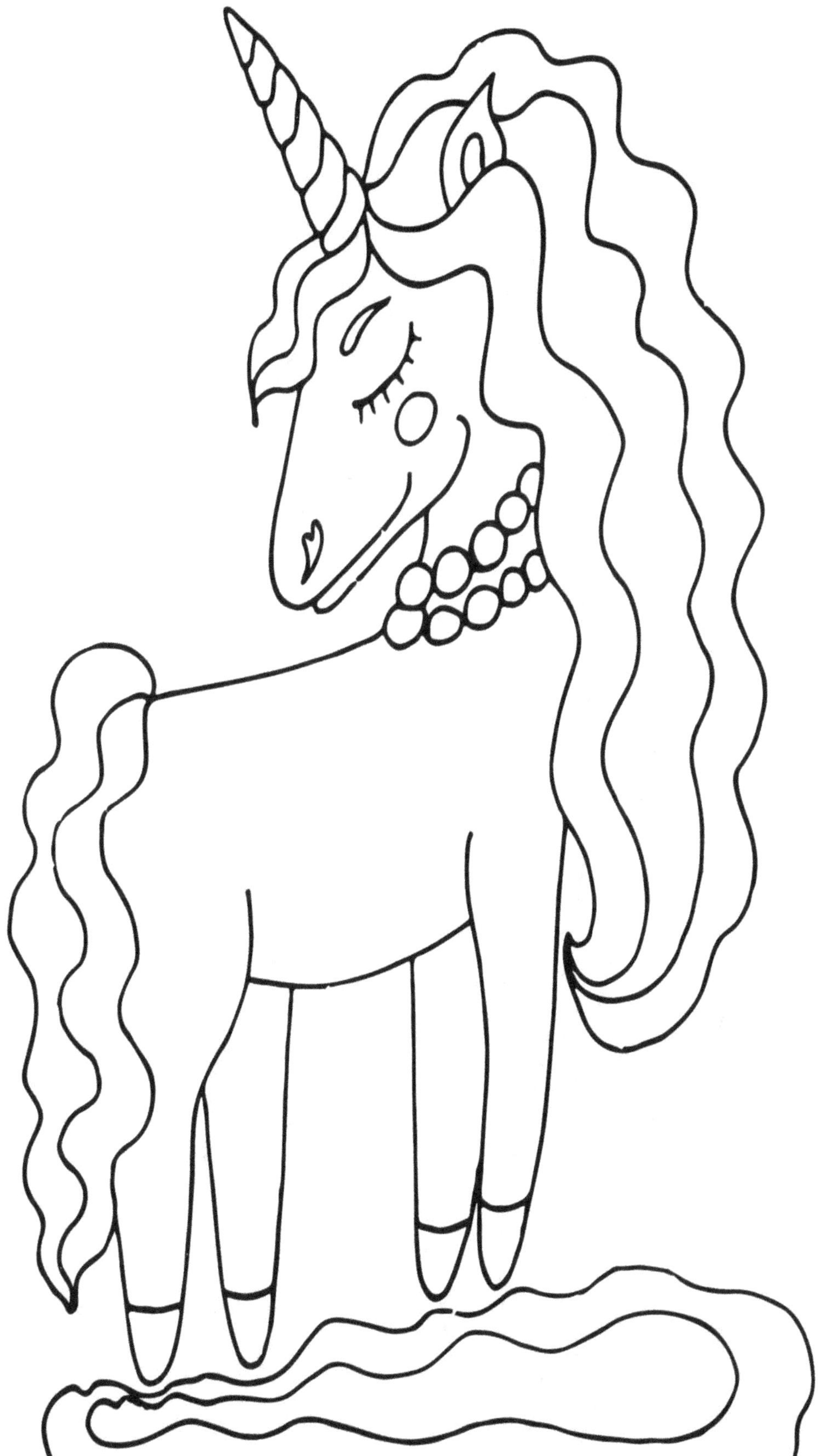

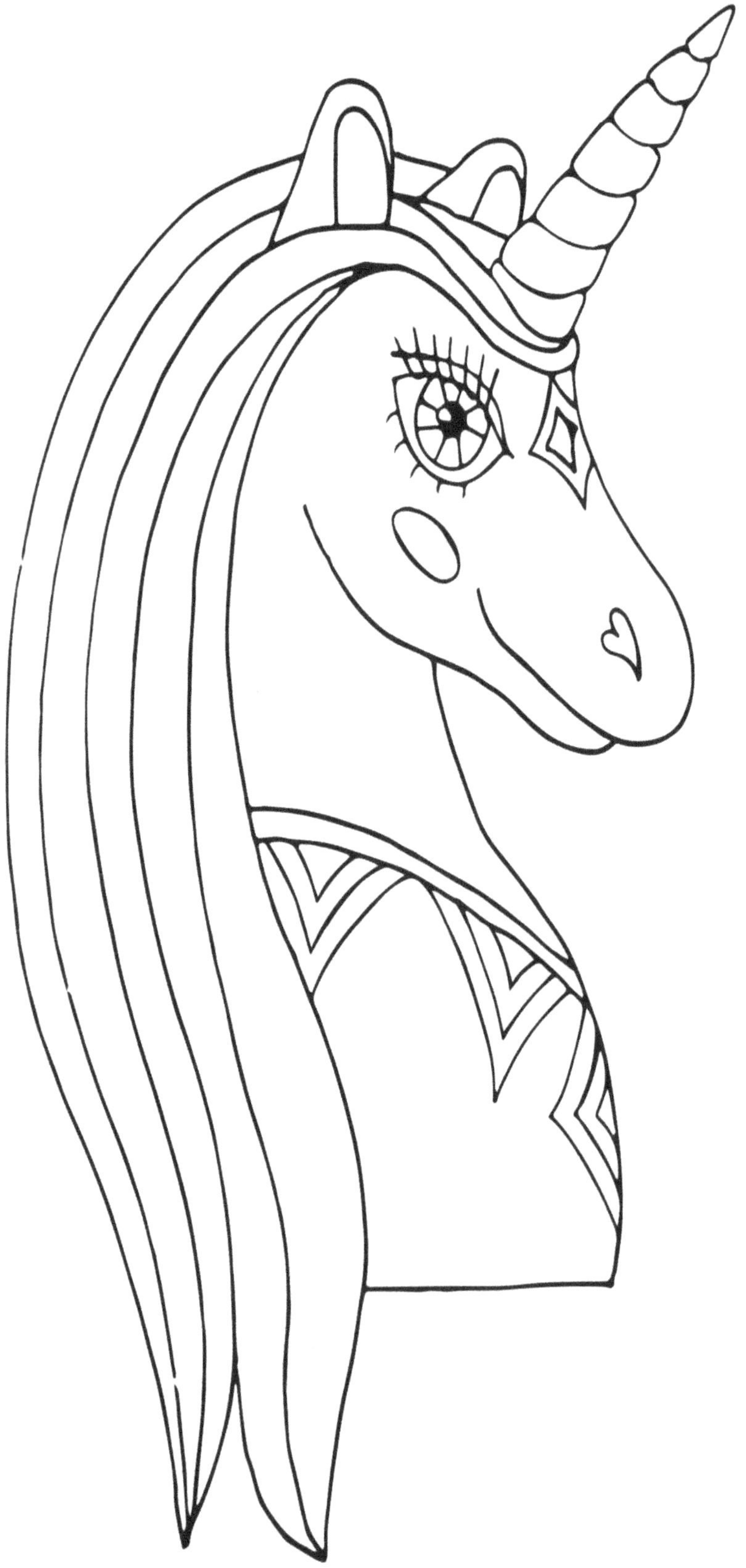

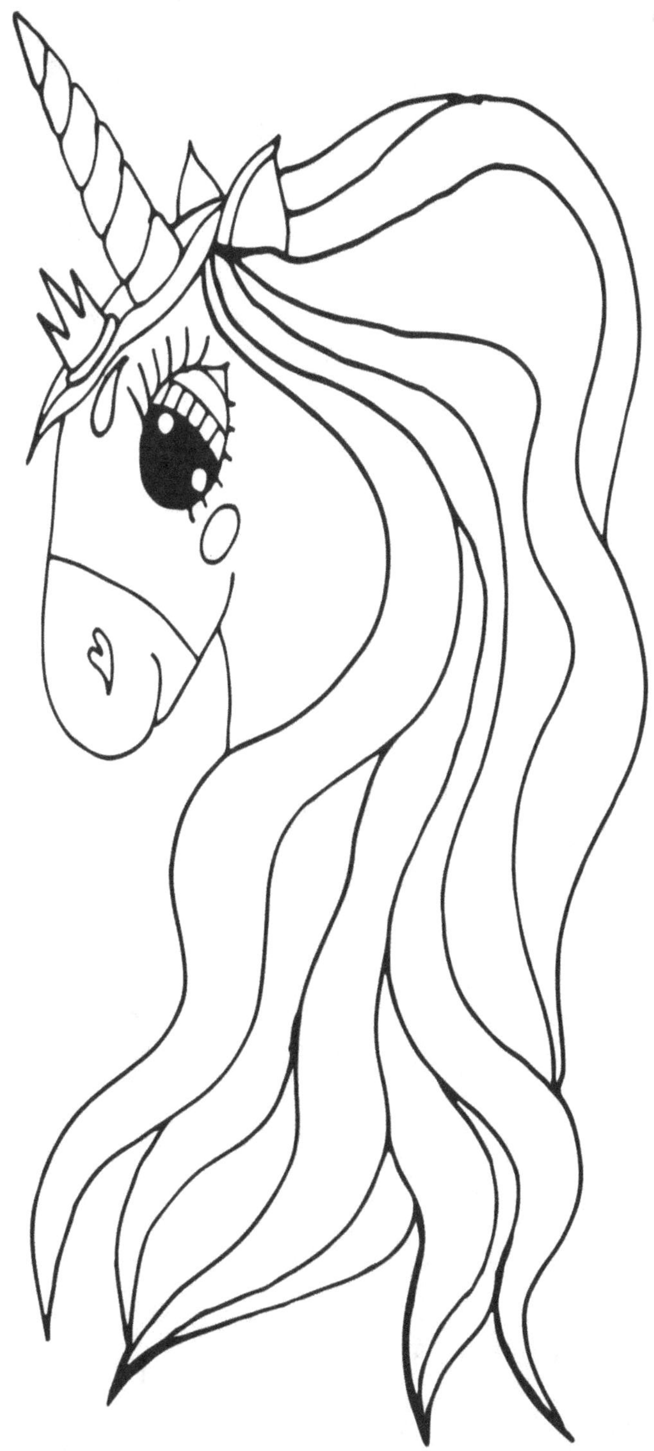

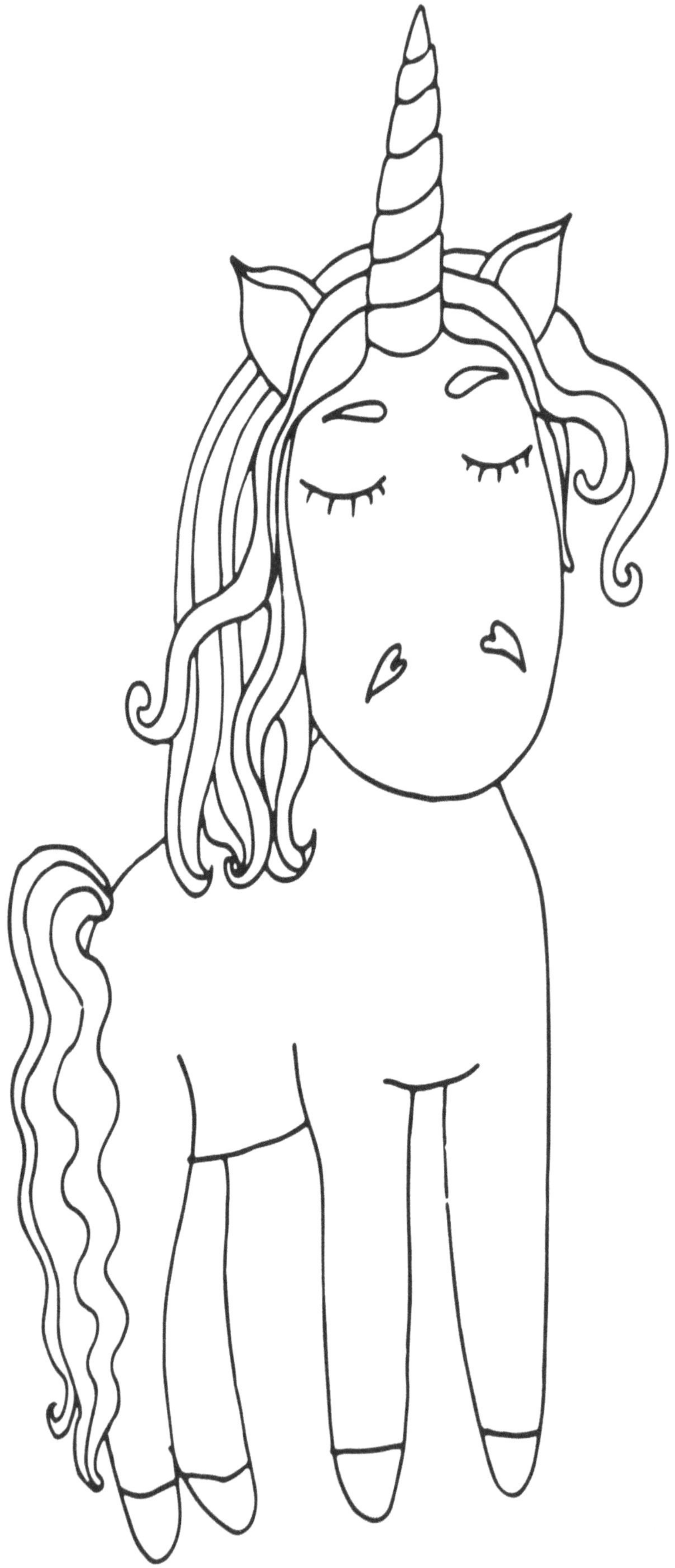

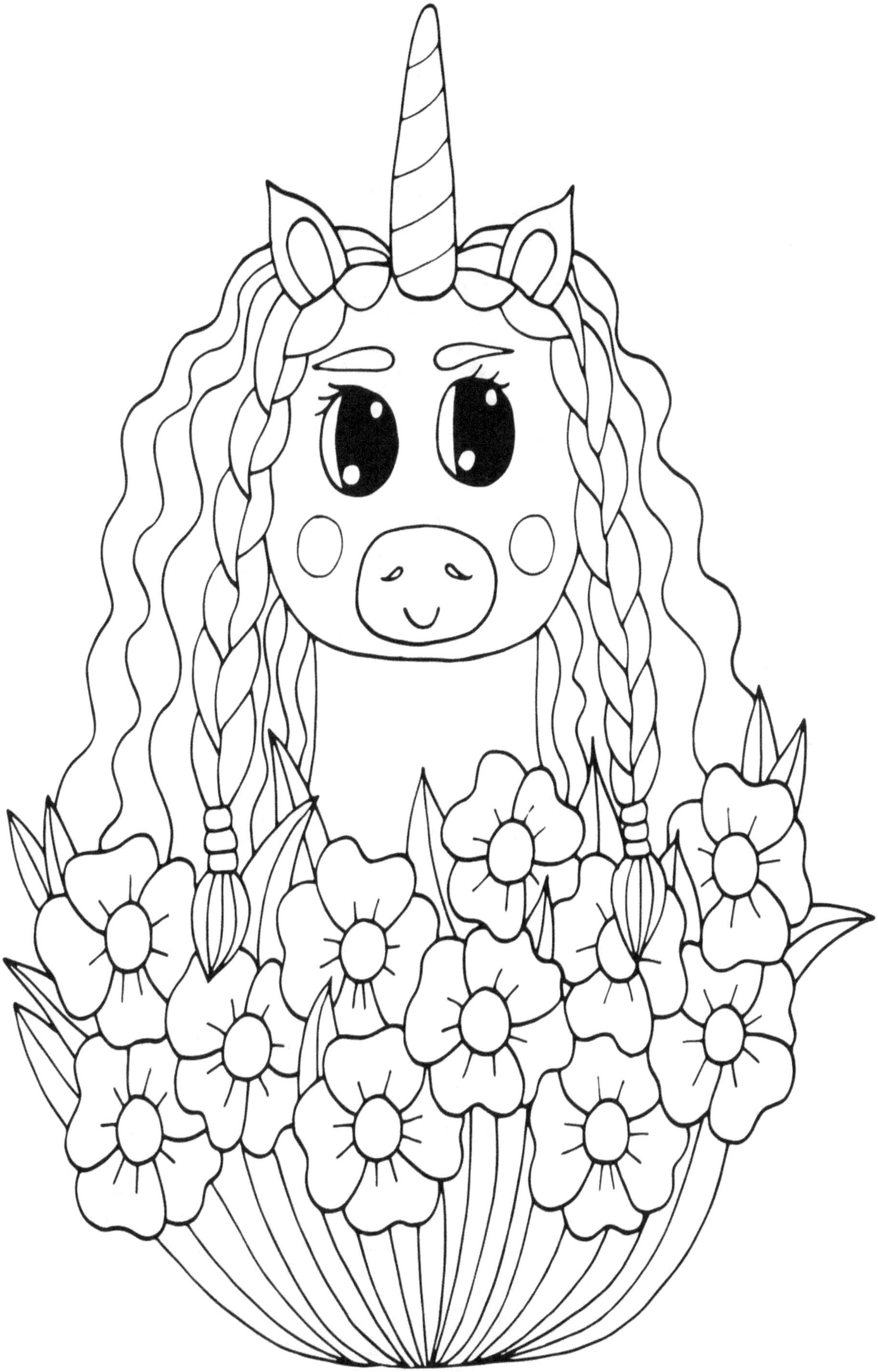

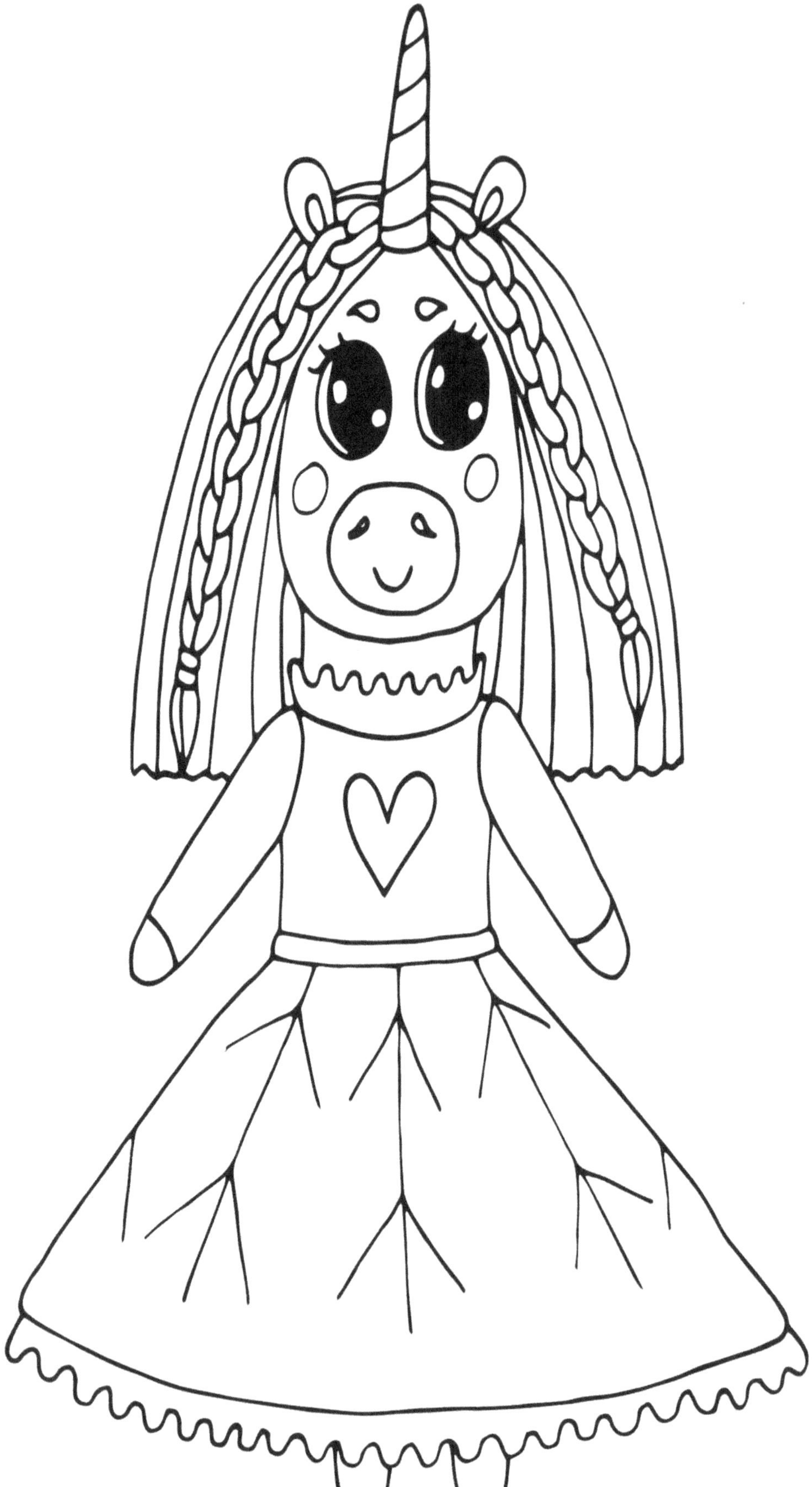

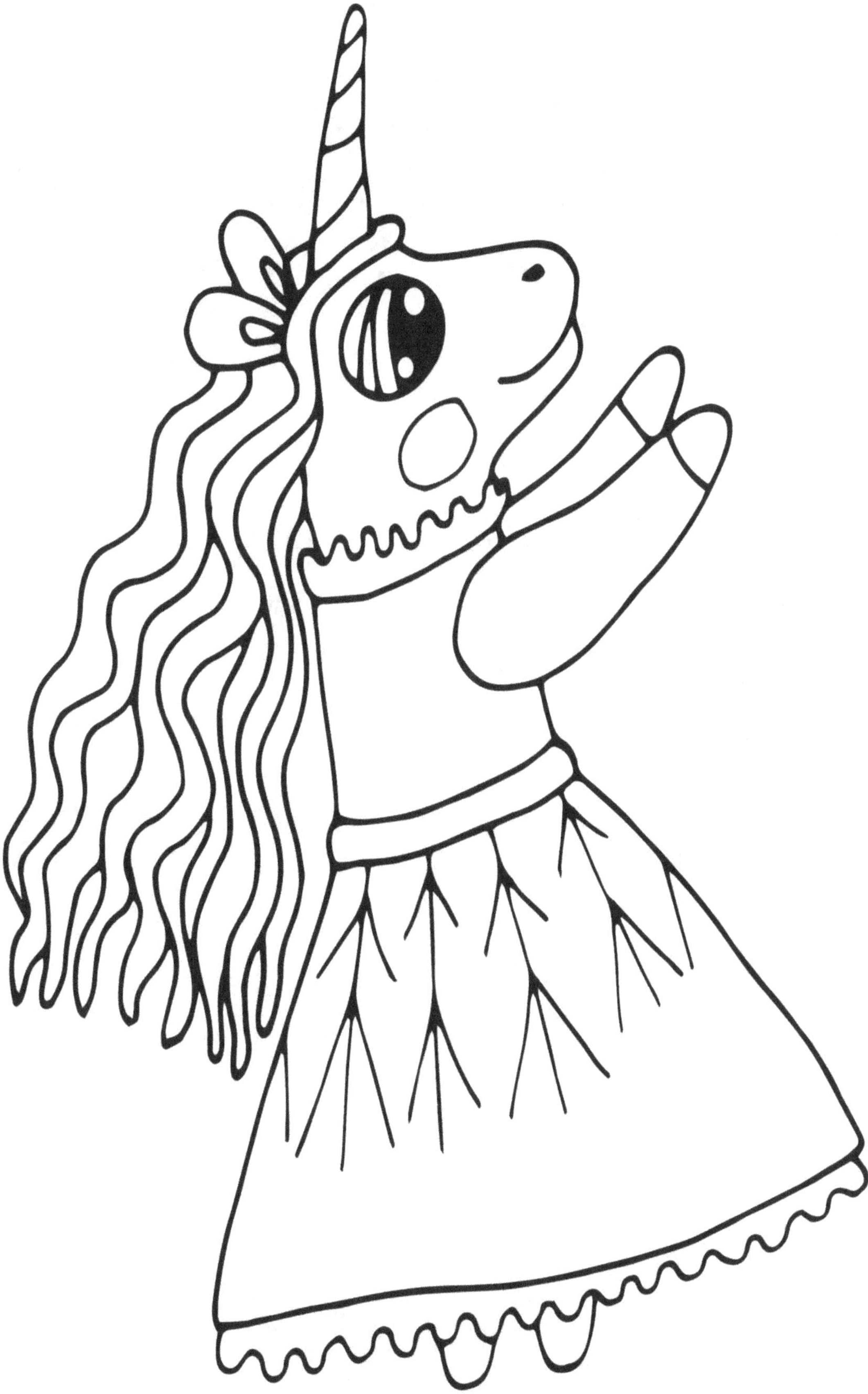

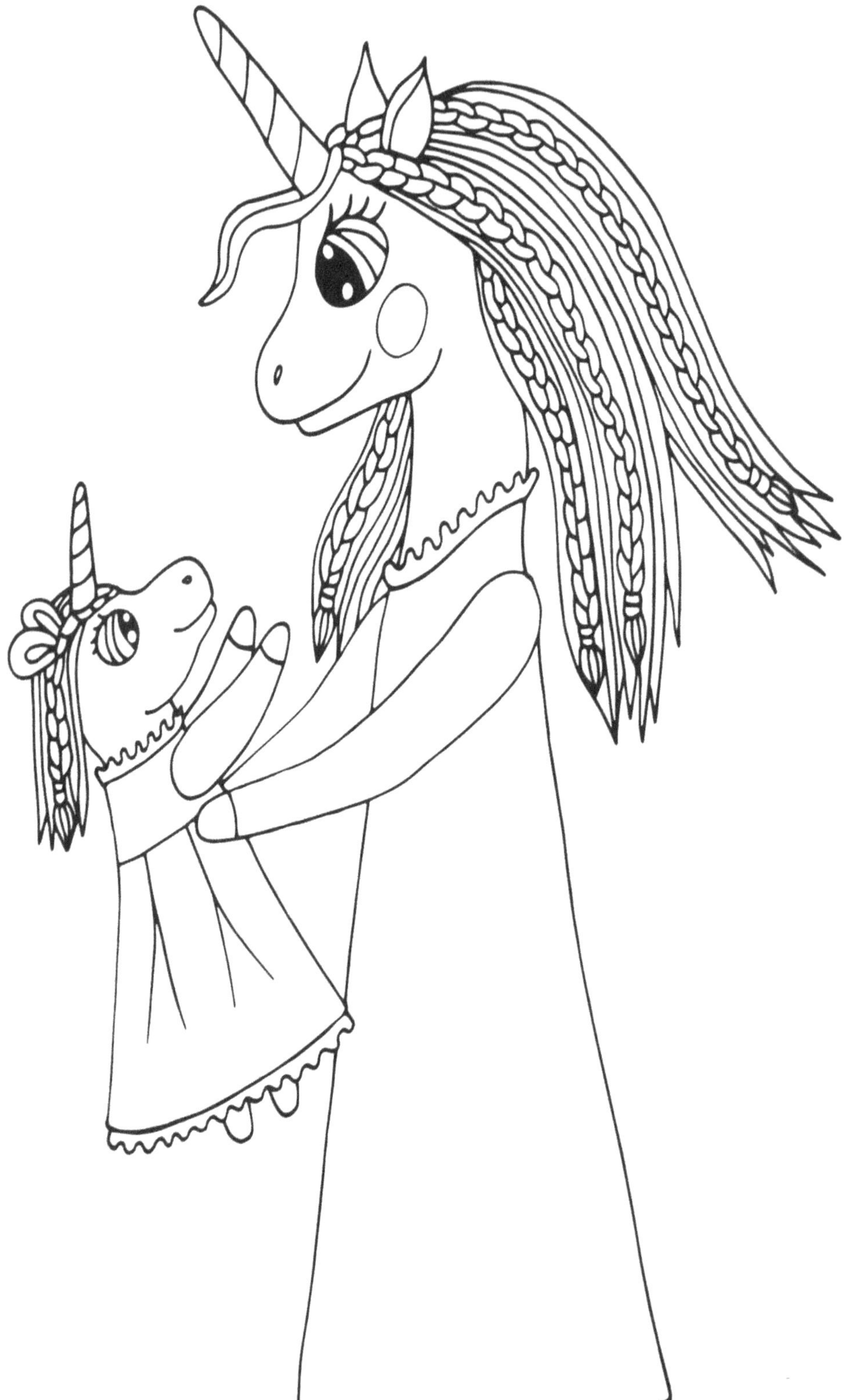

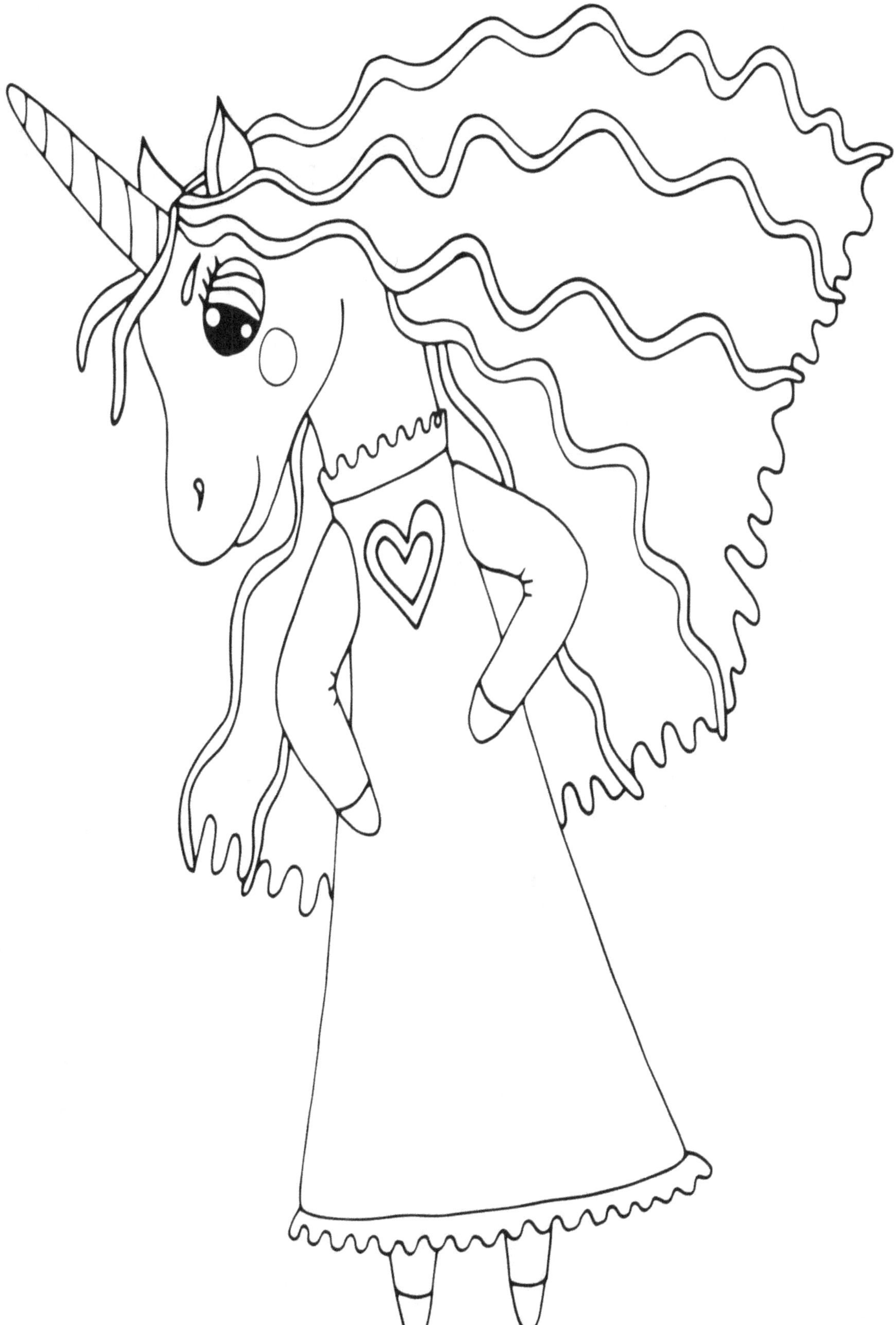

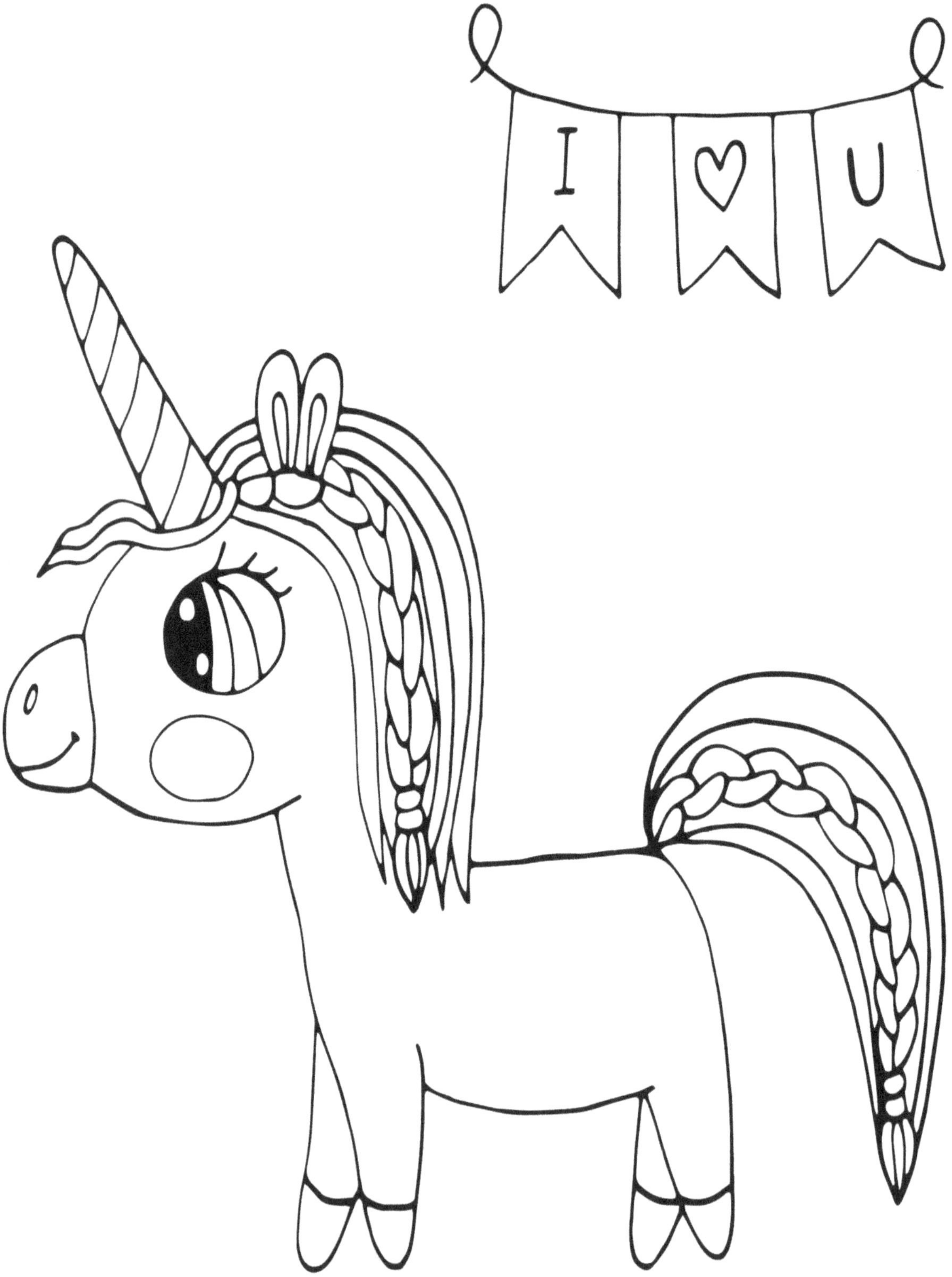
I ♡ U

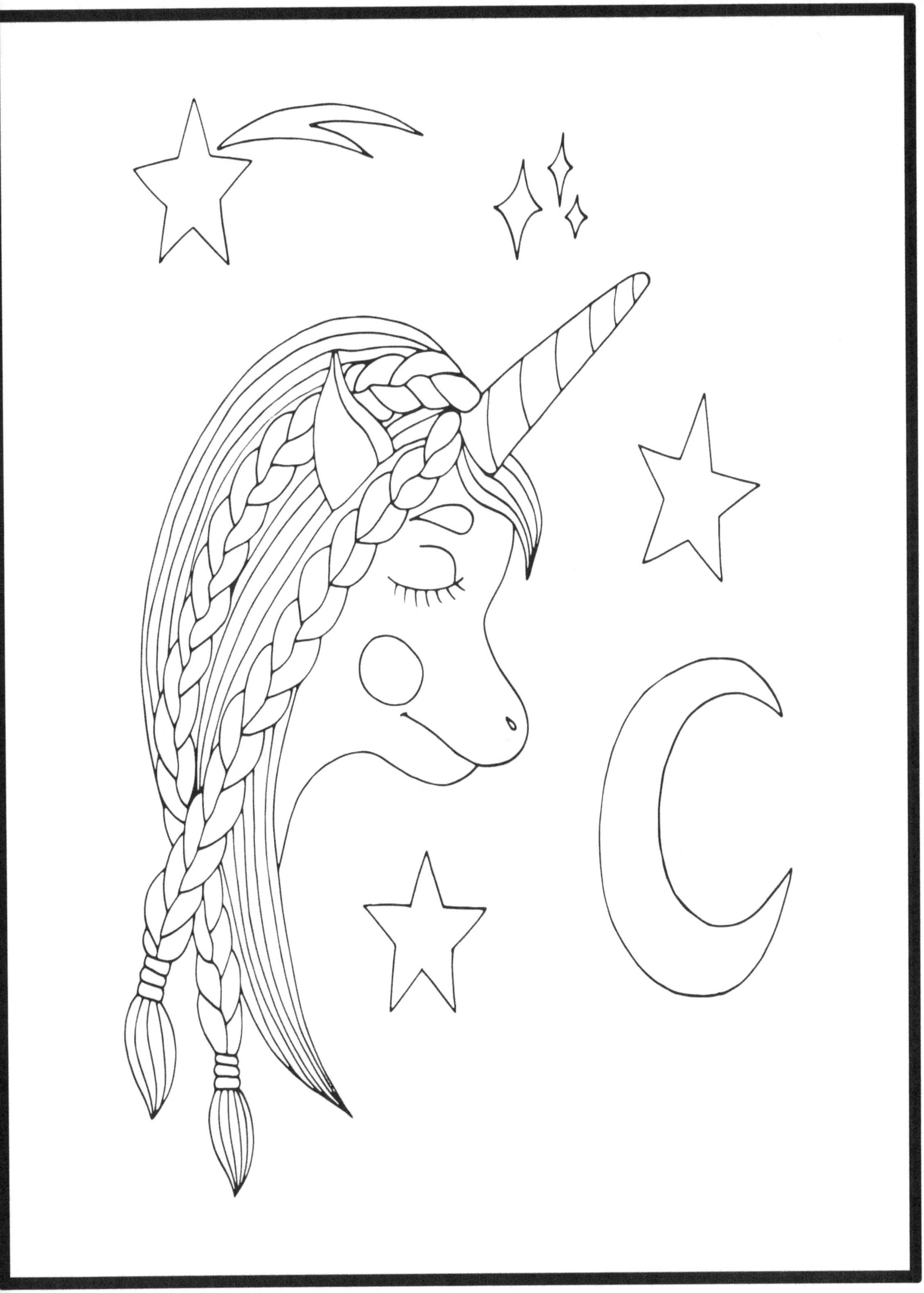

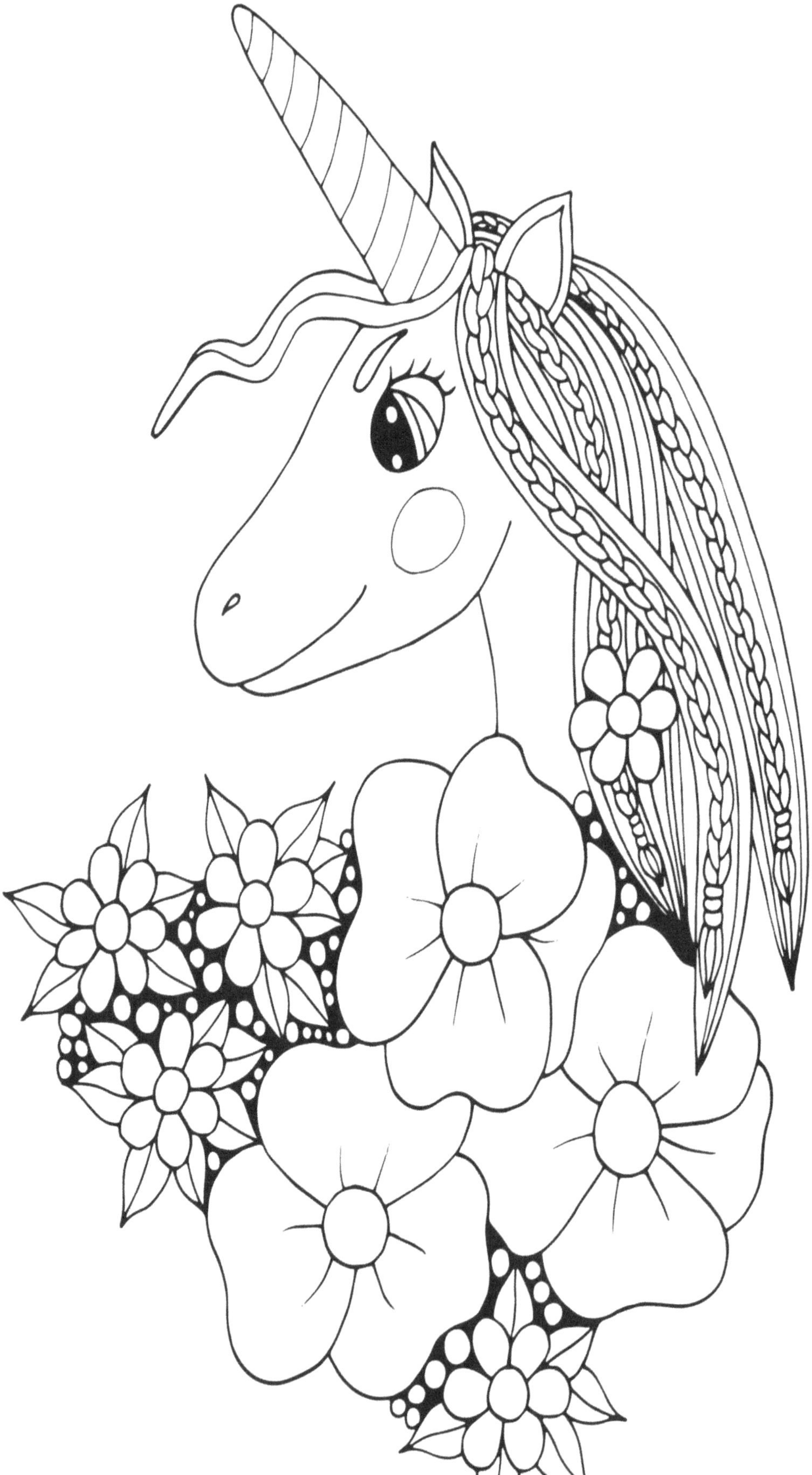

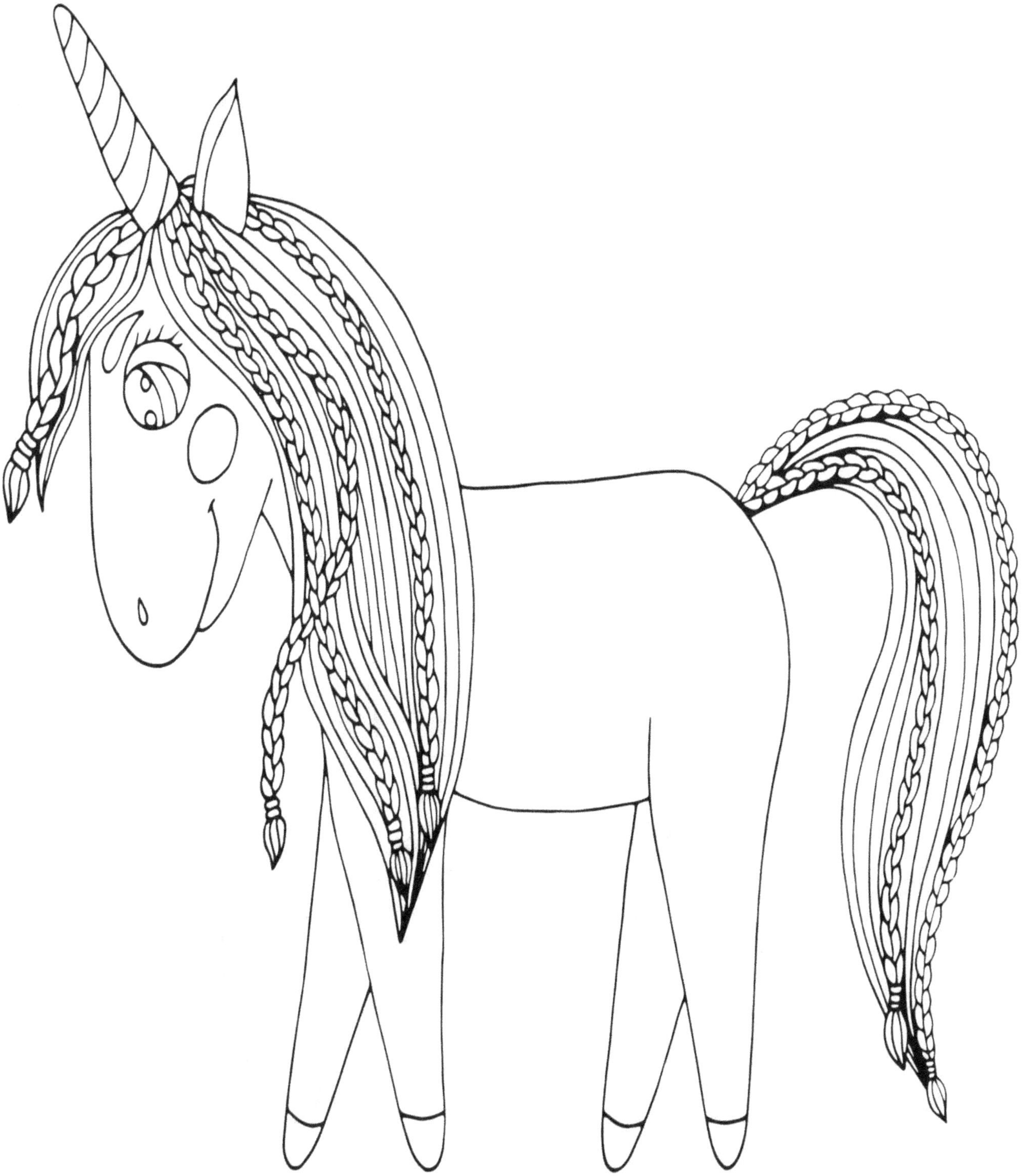

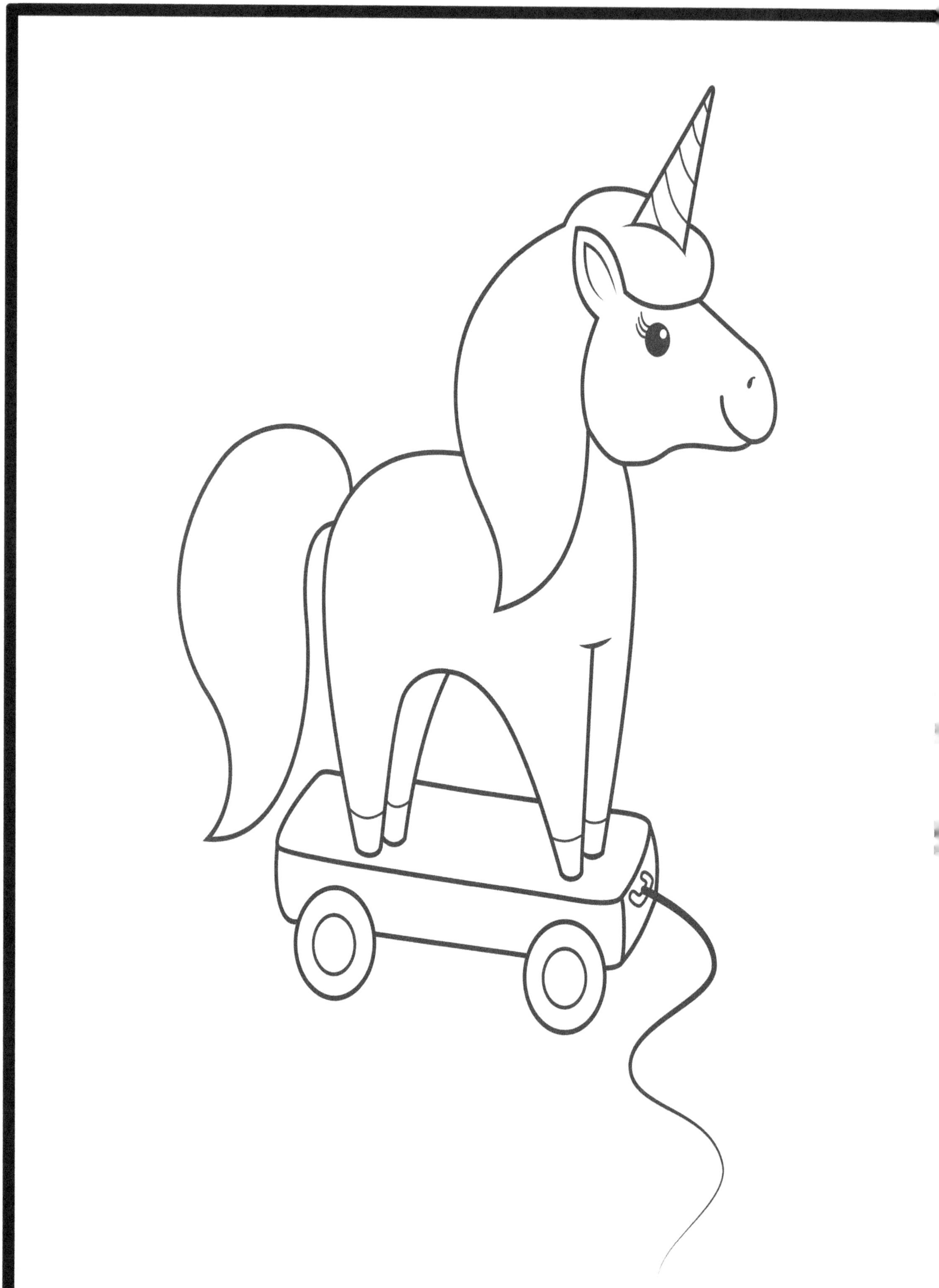

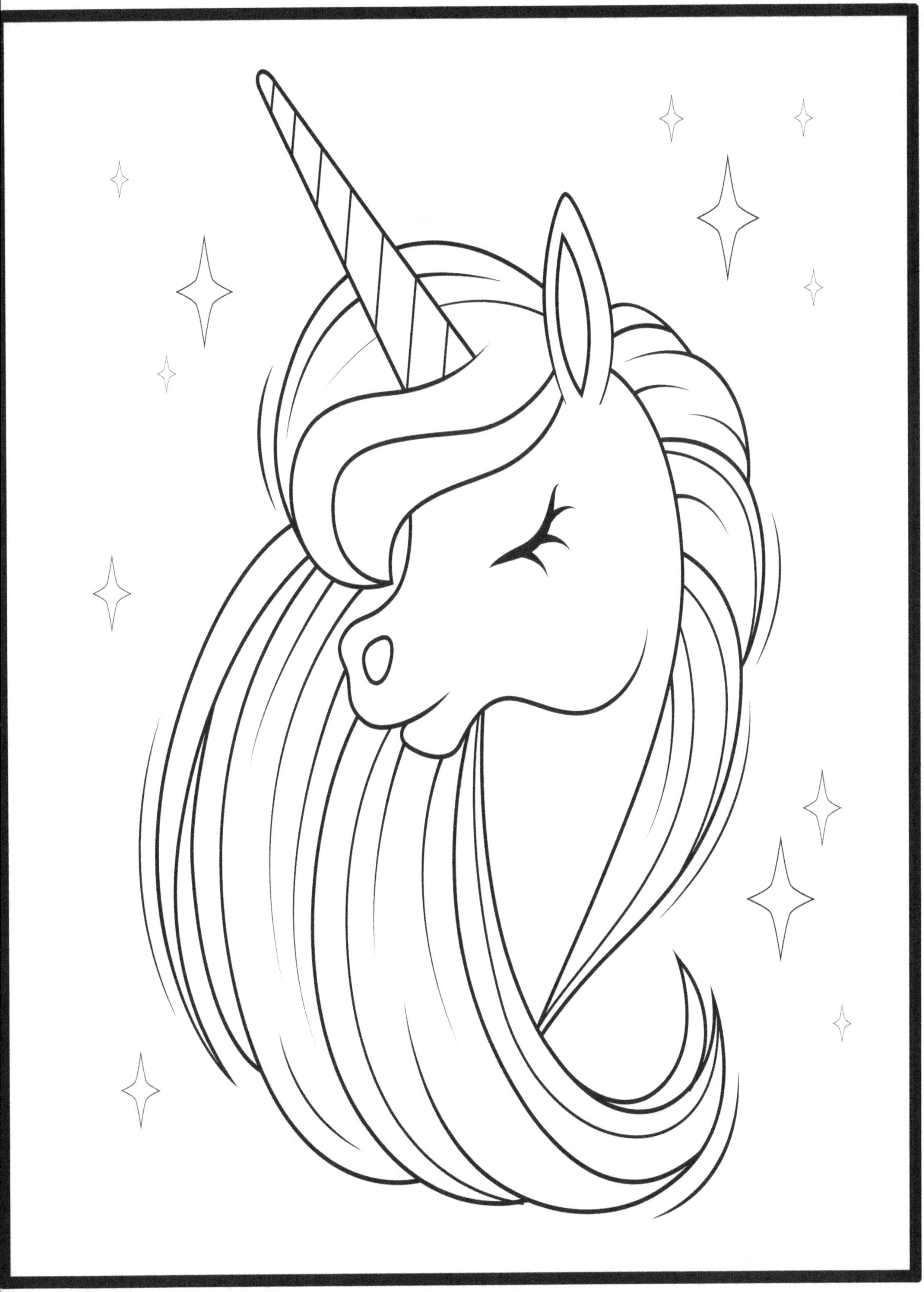

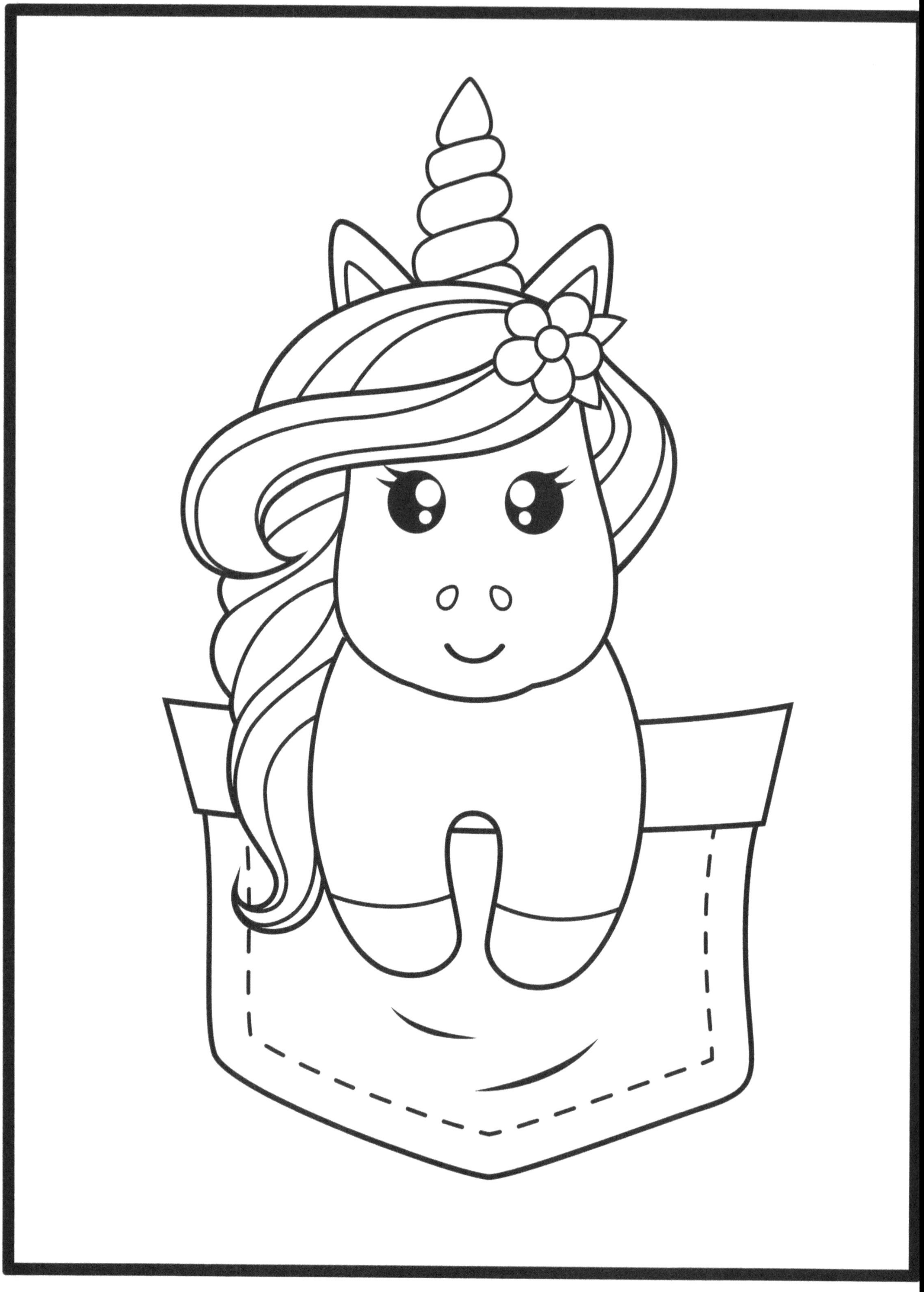

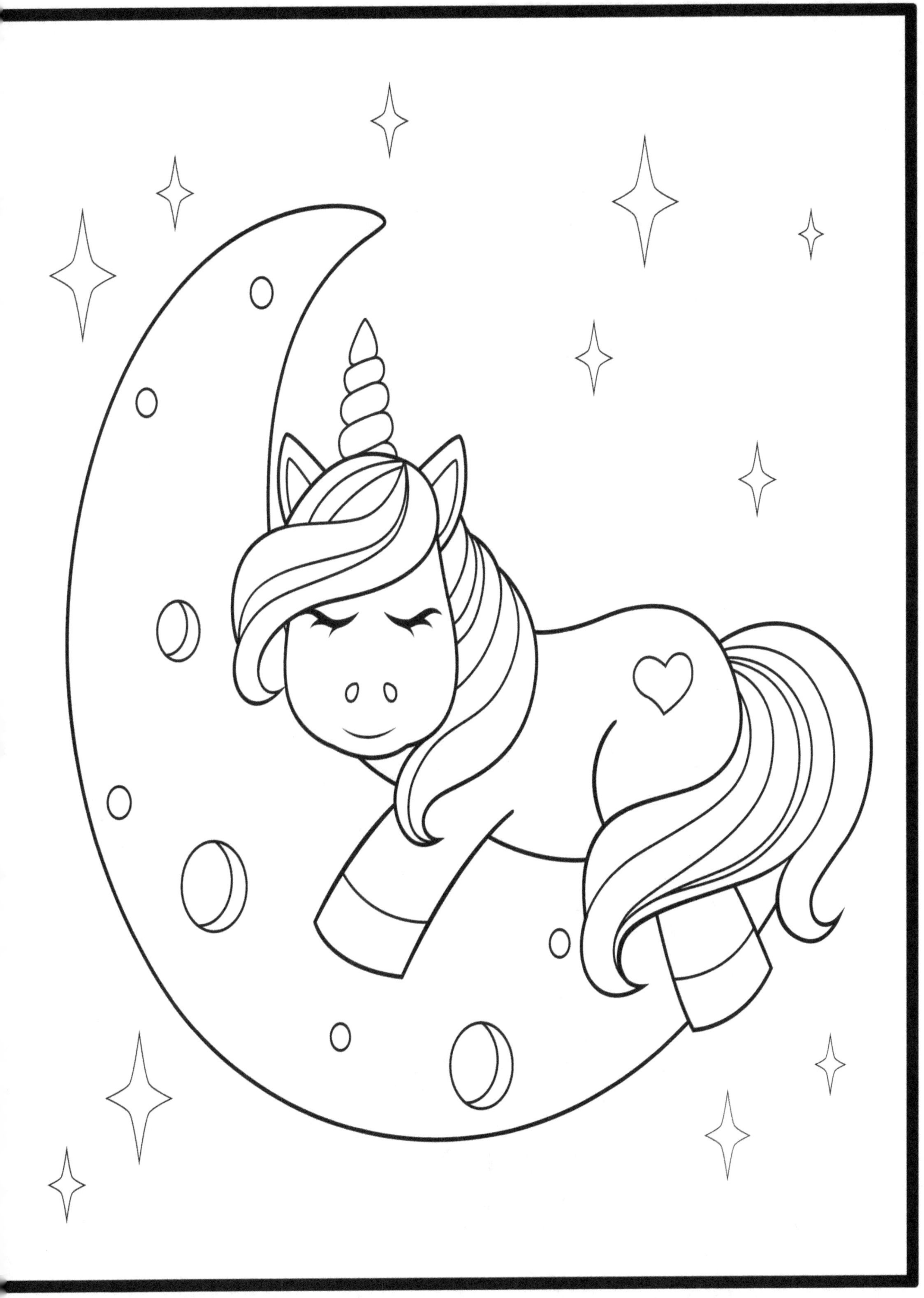

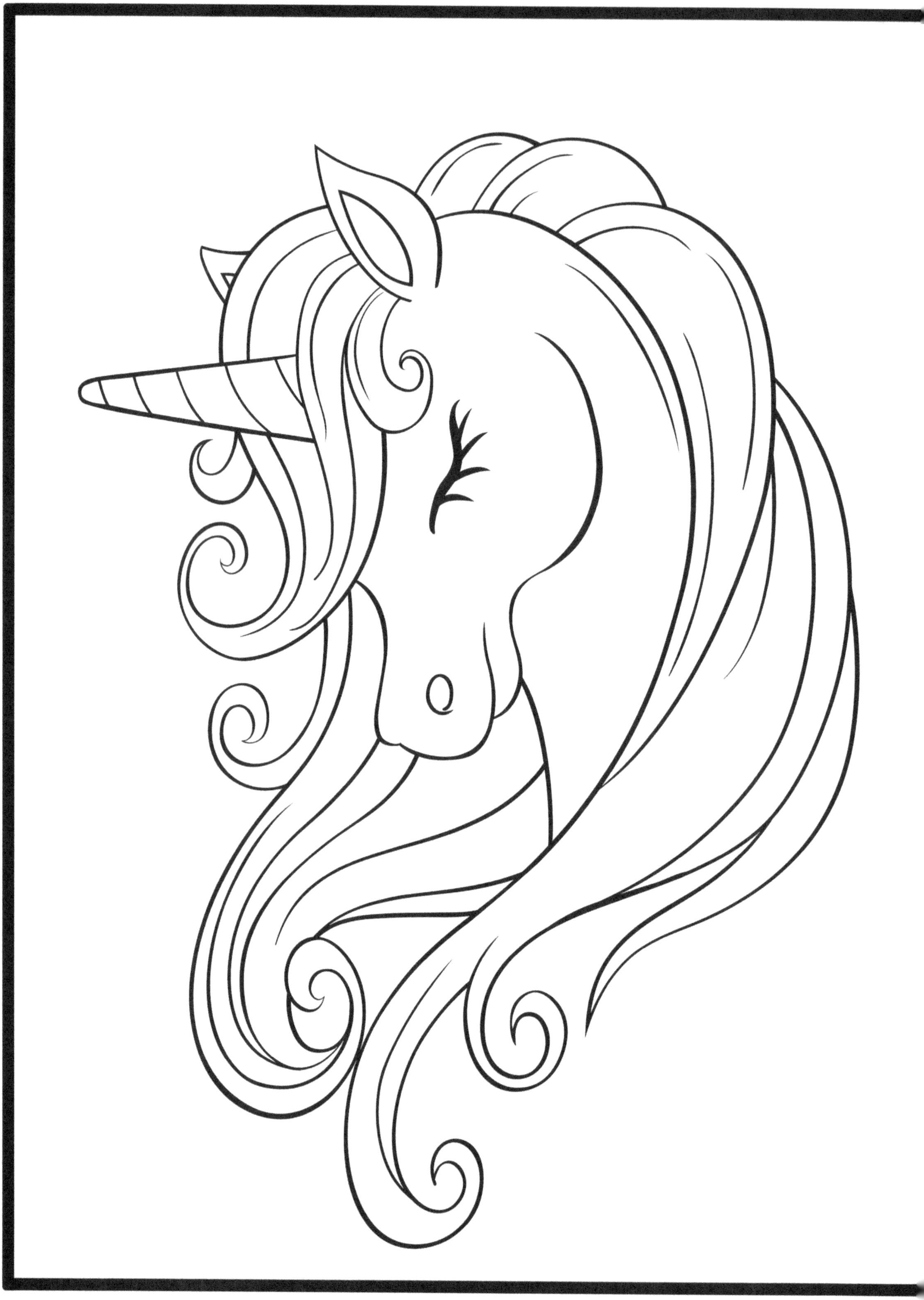

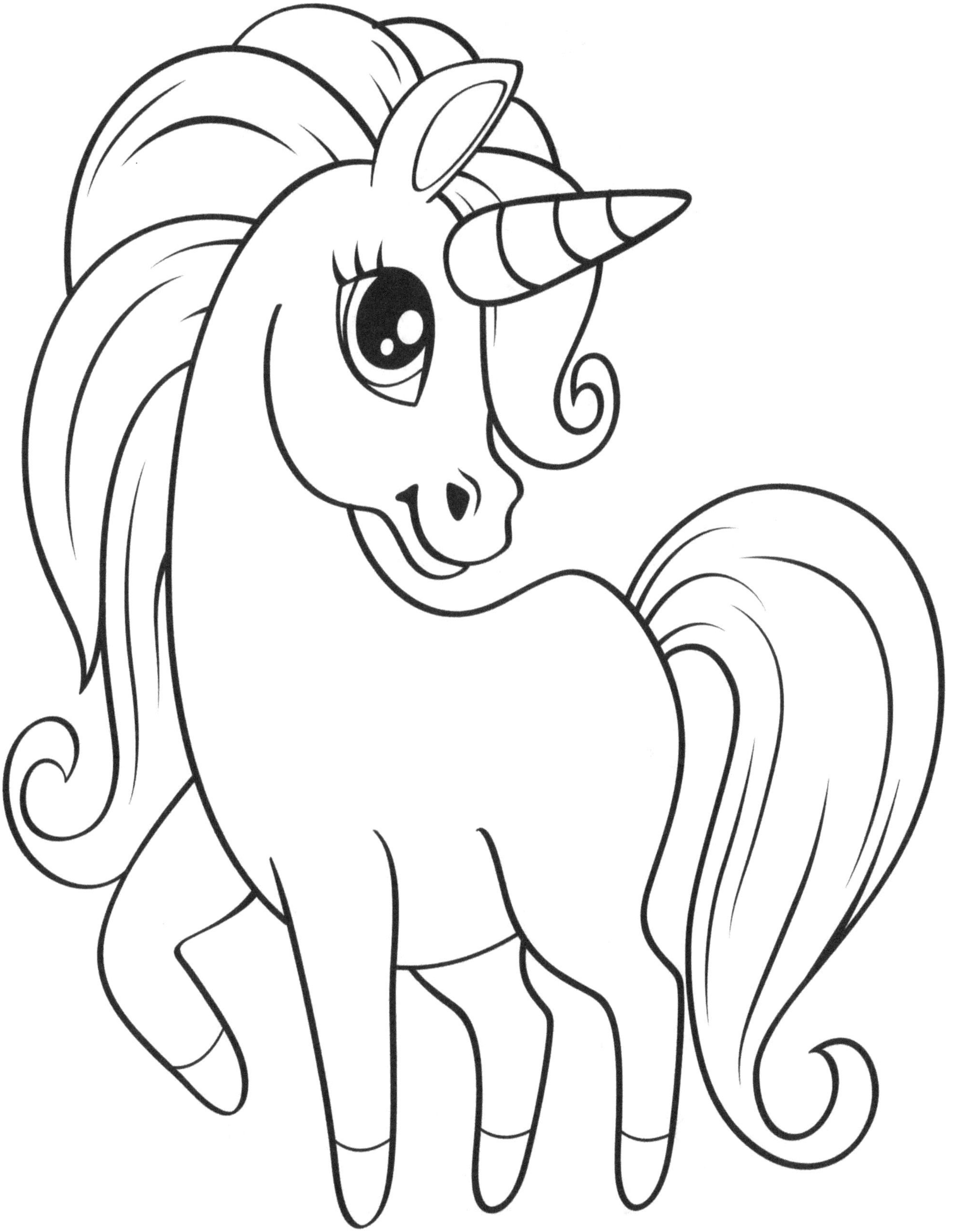

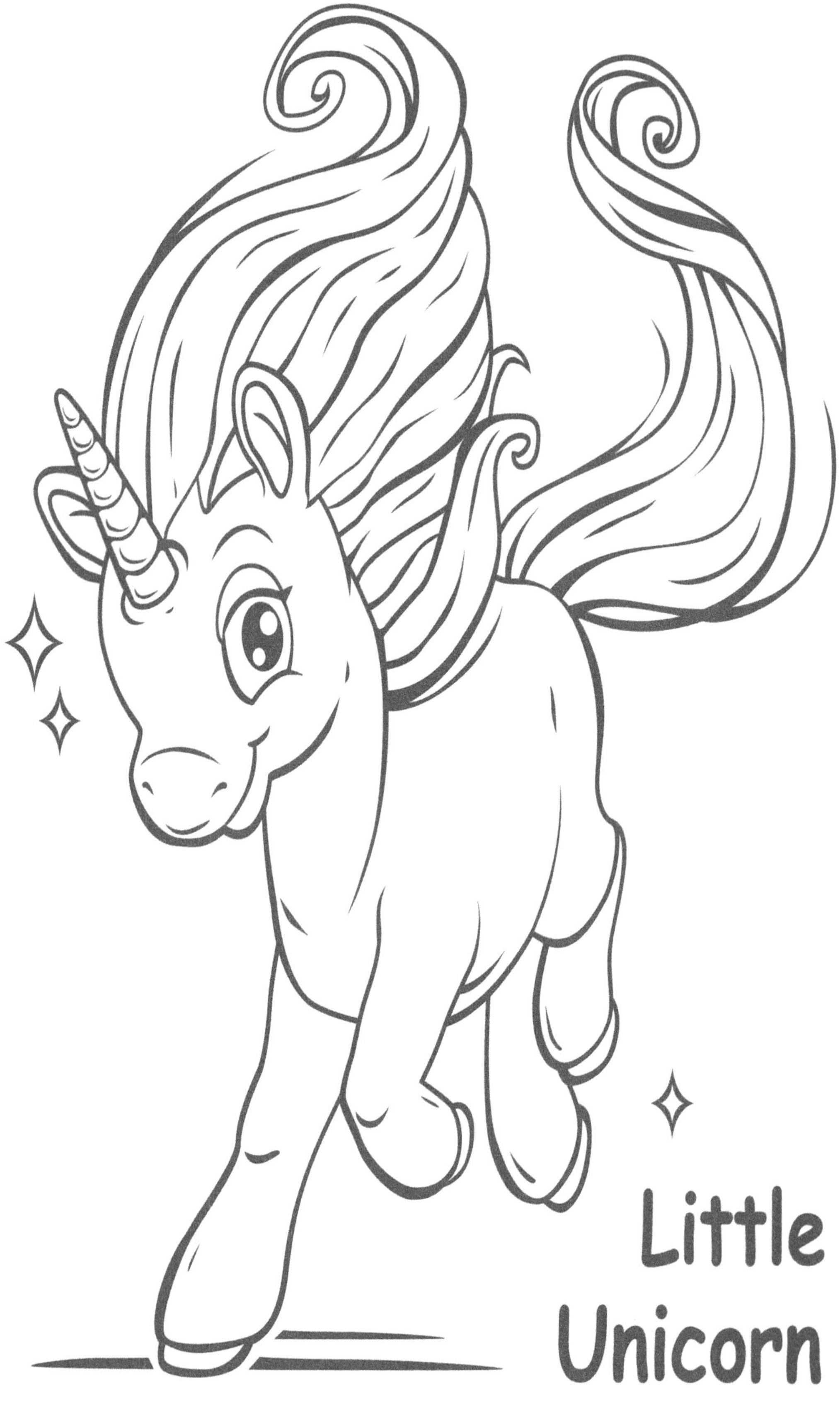

Little
Unicorn

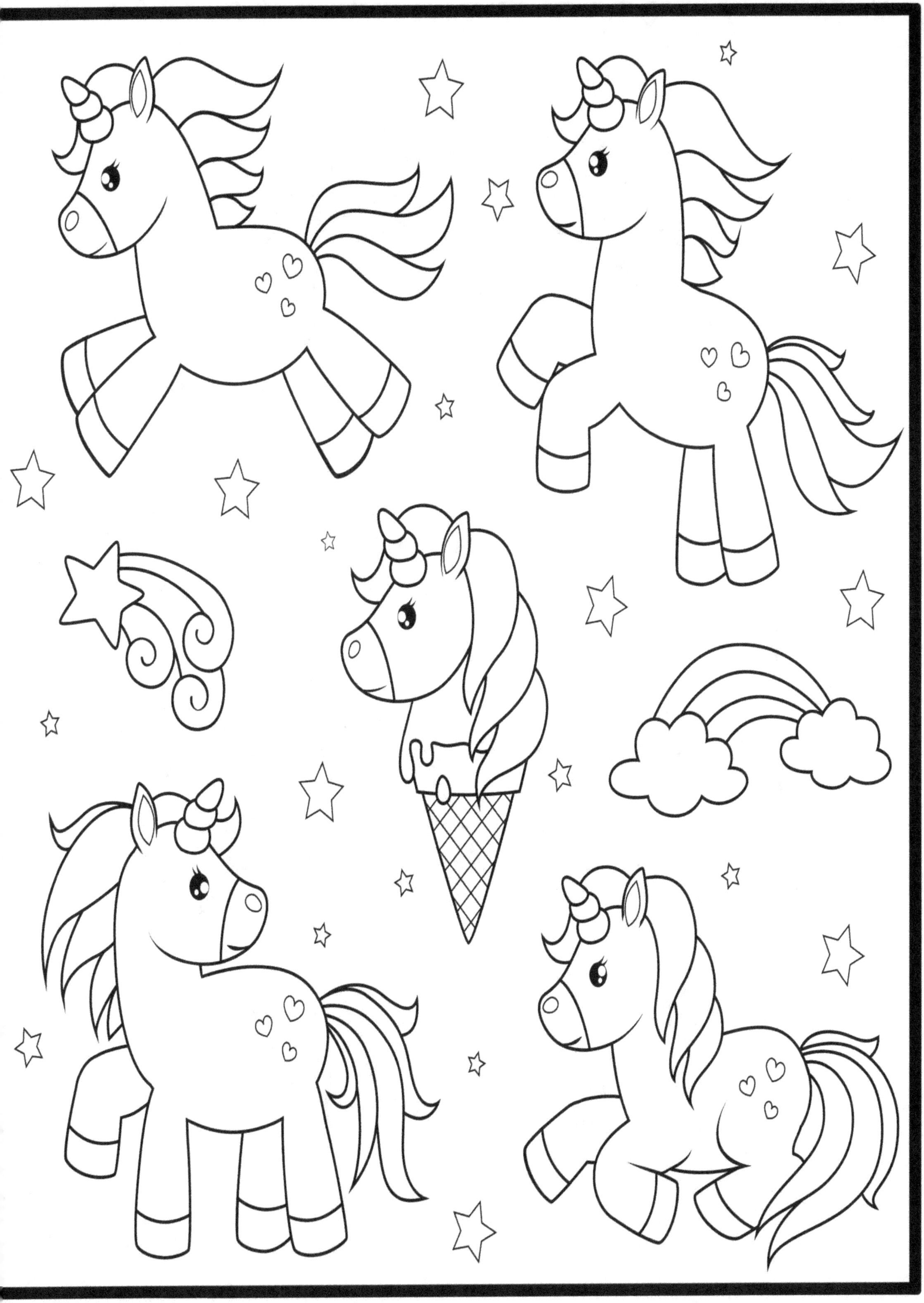

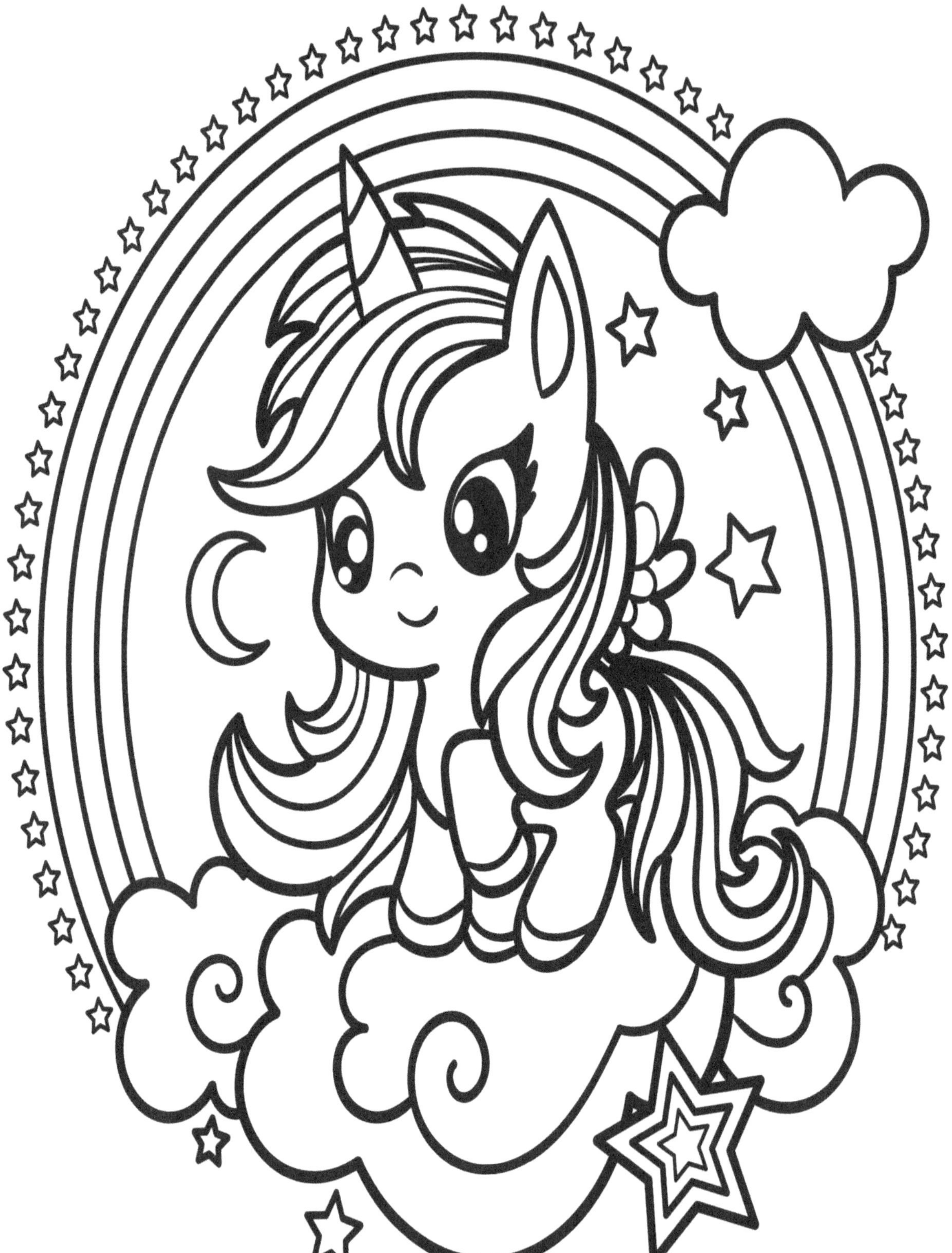

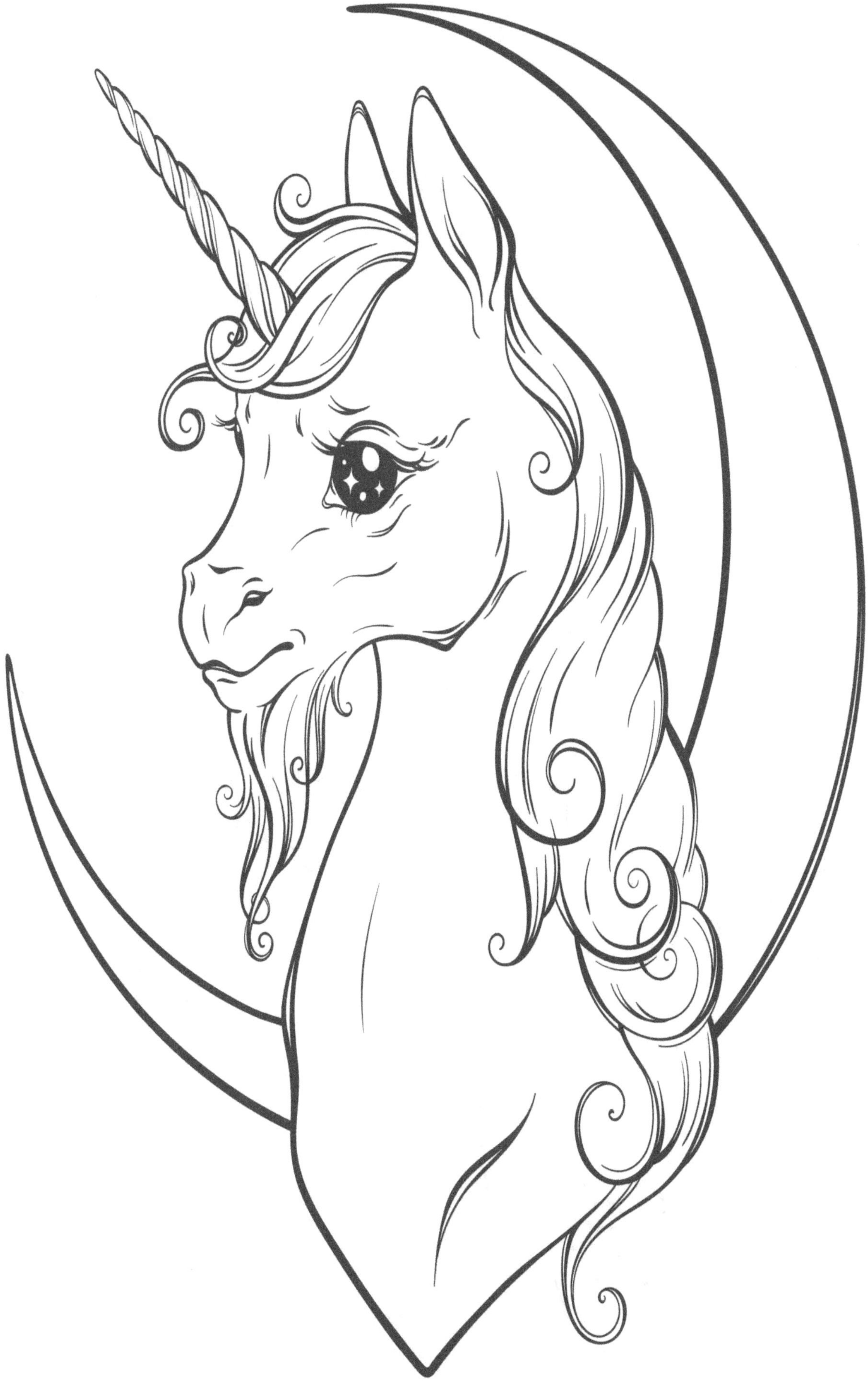

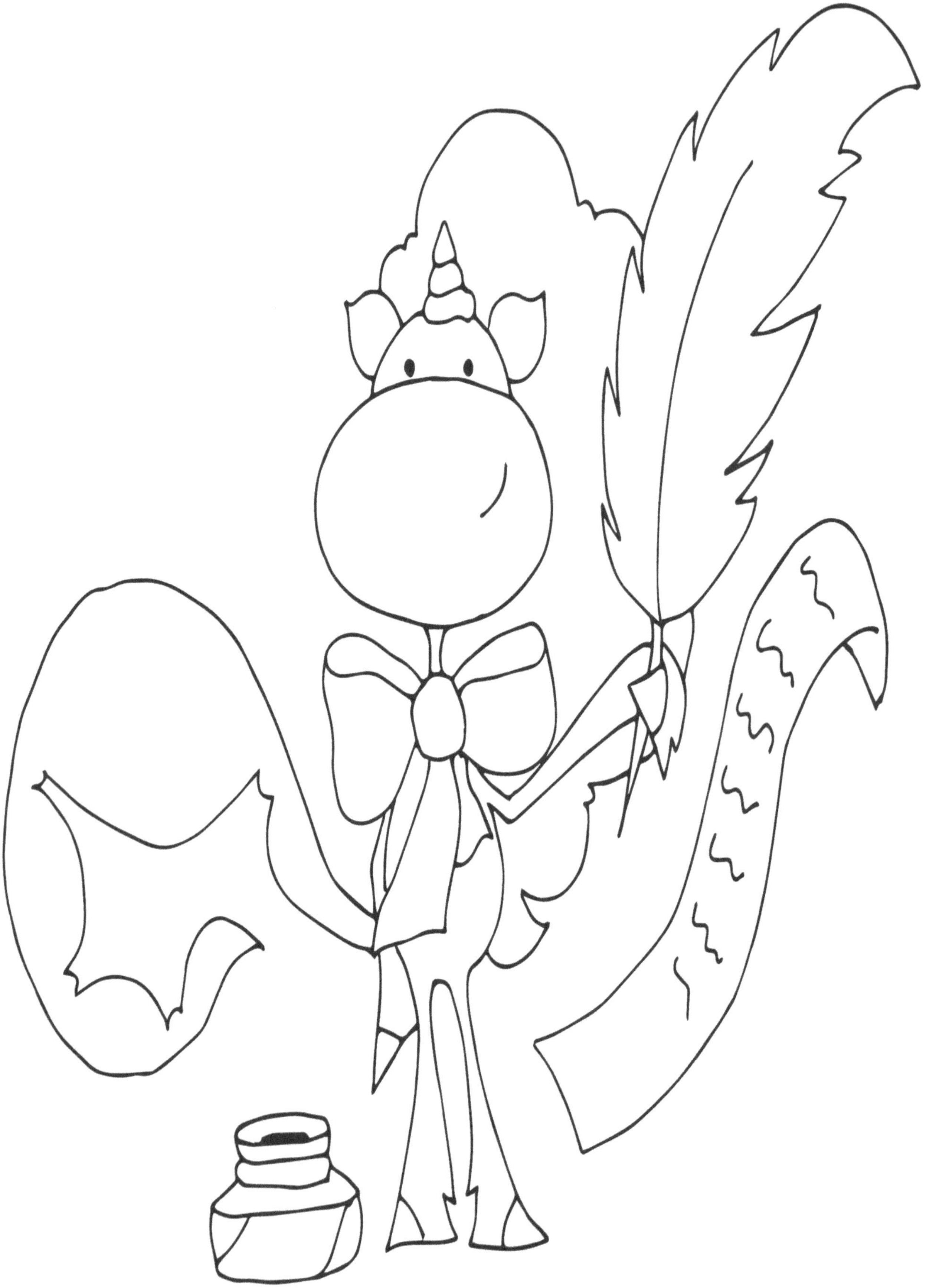

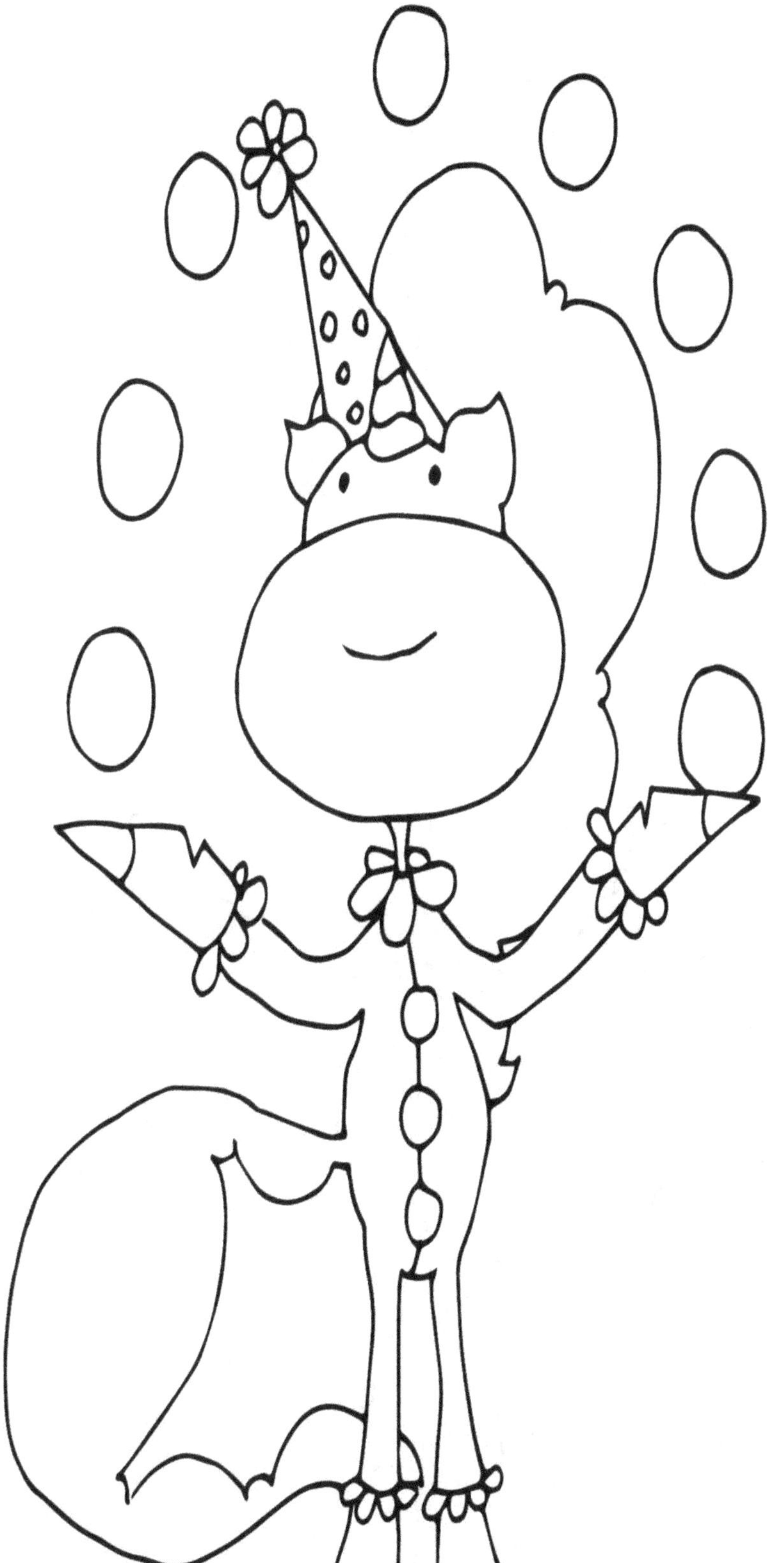

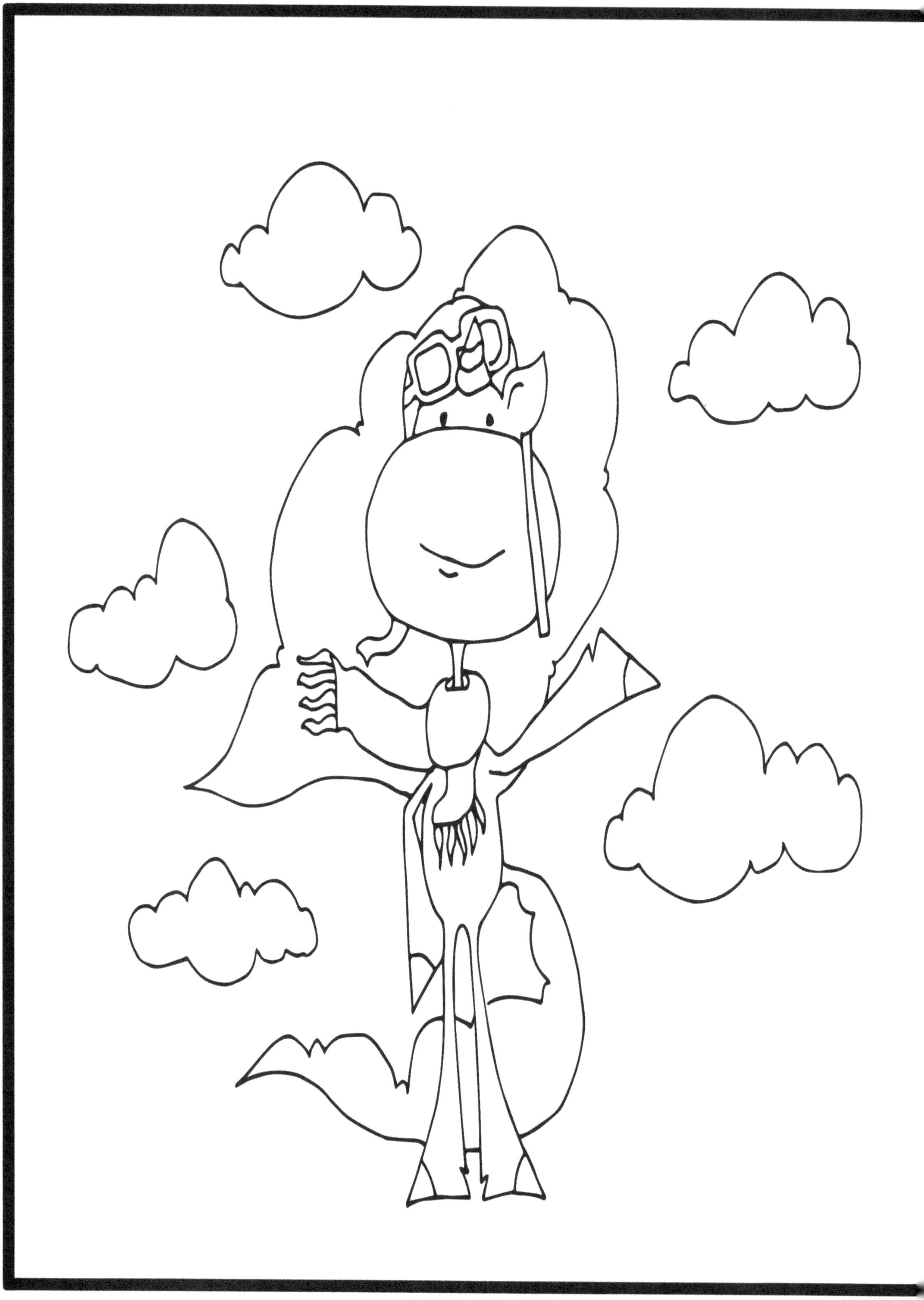

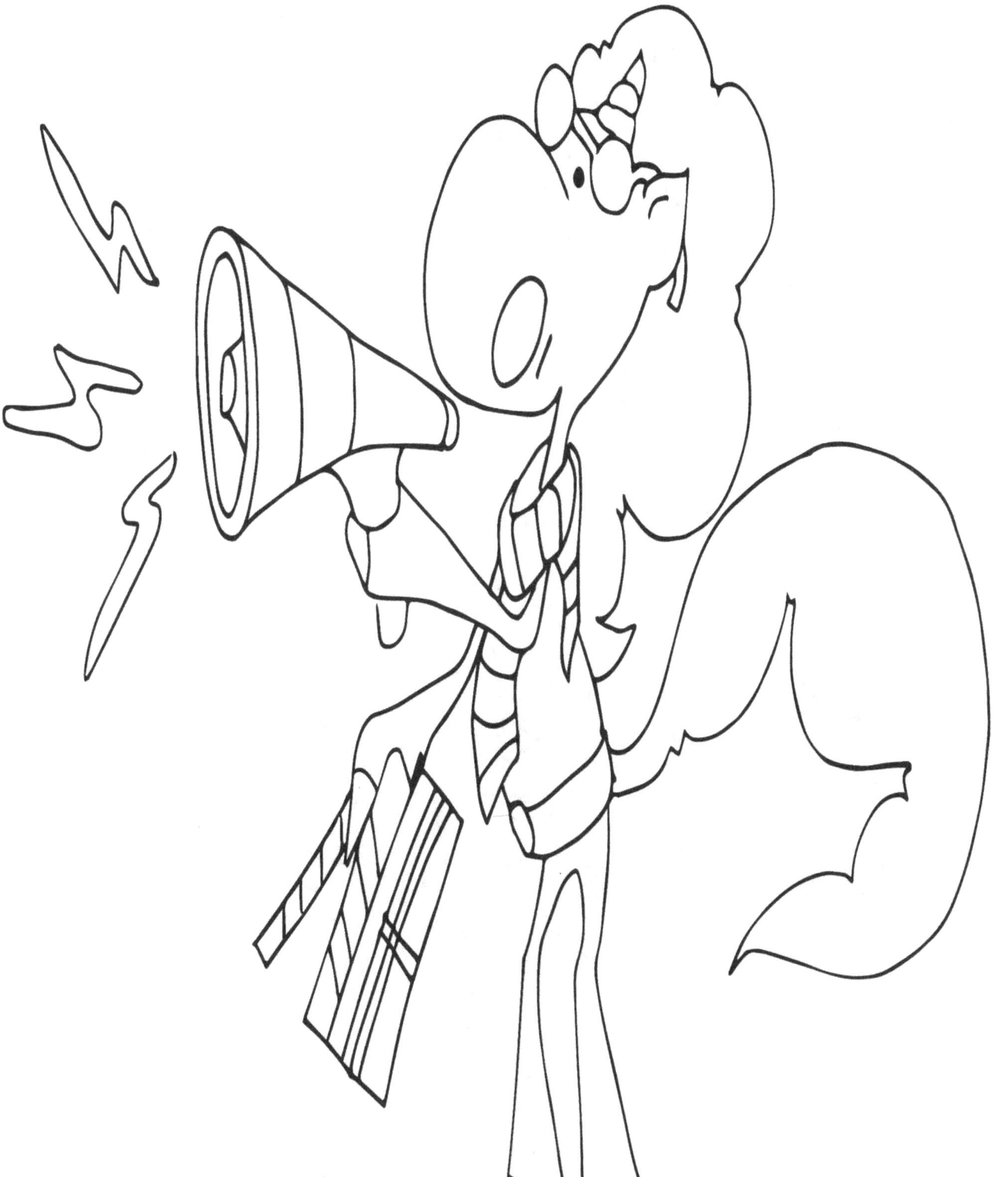

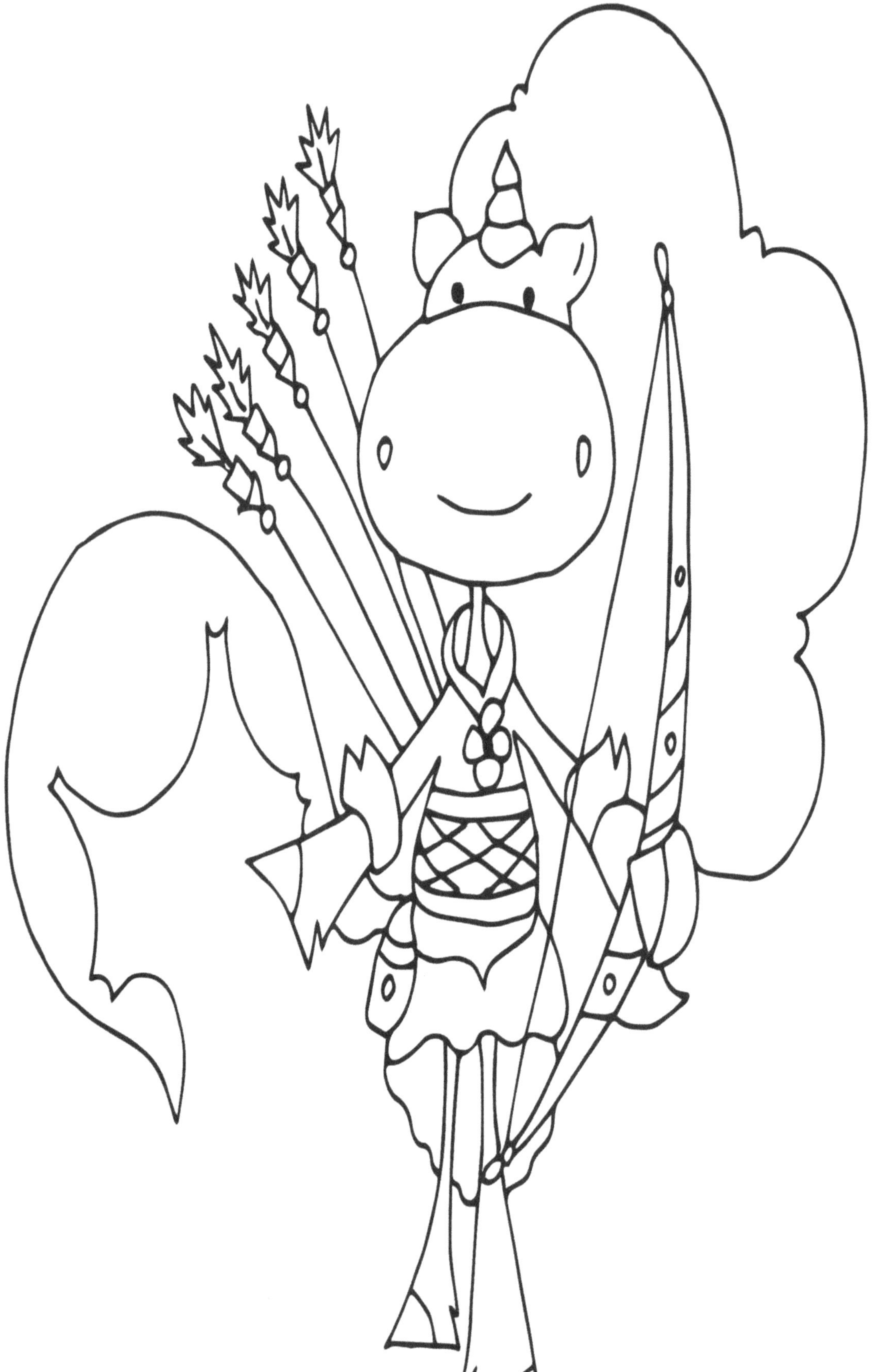

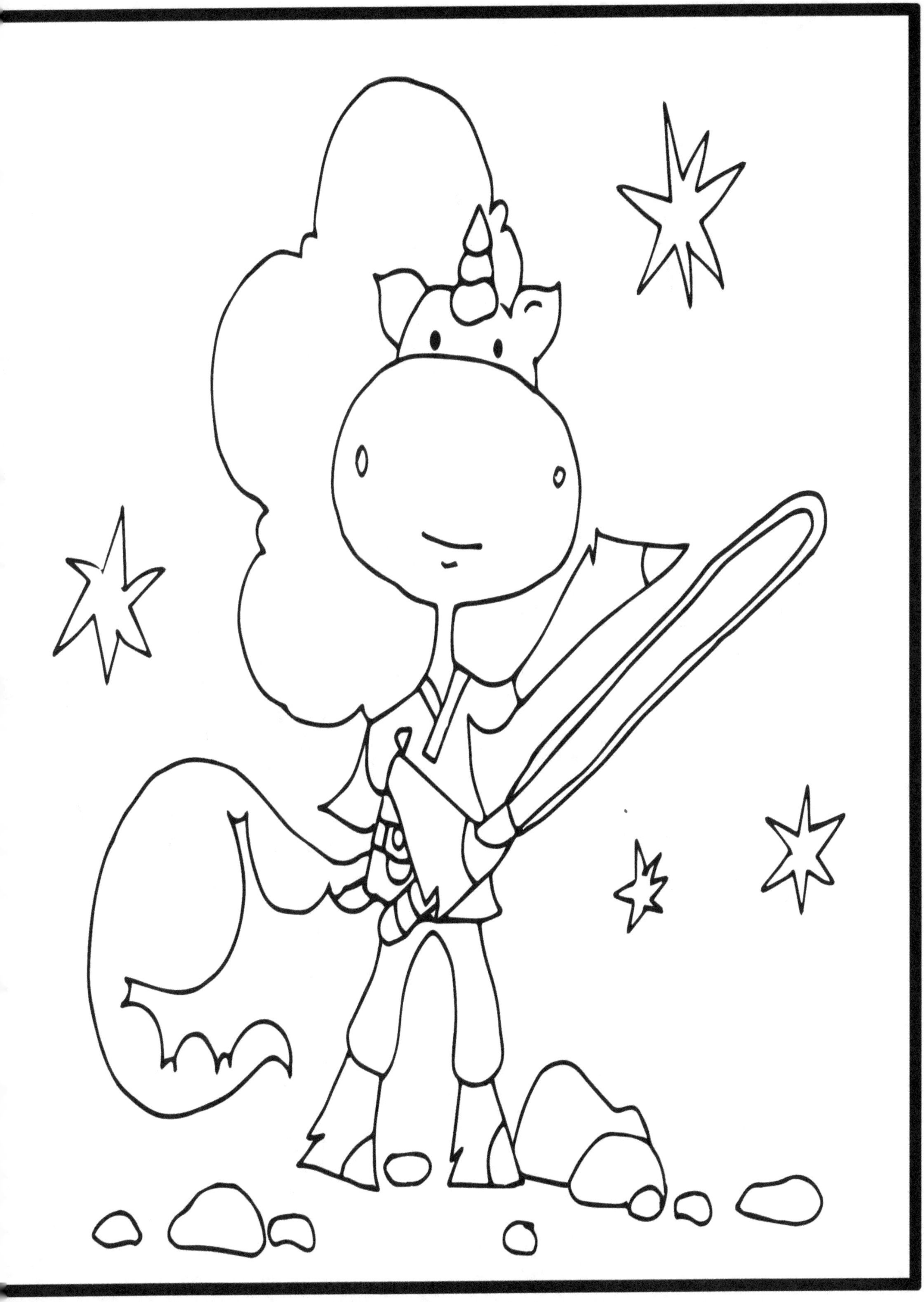

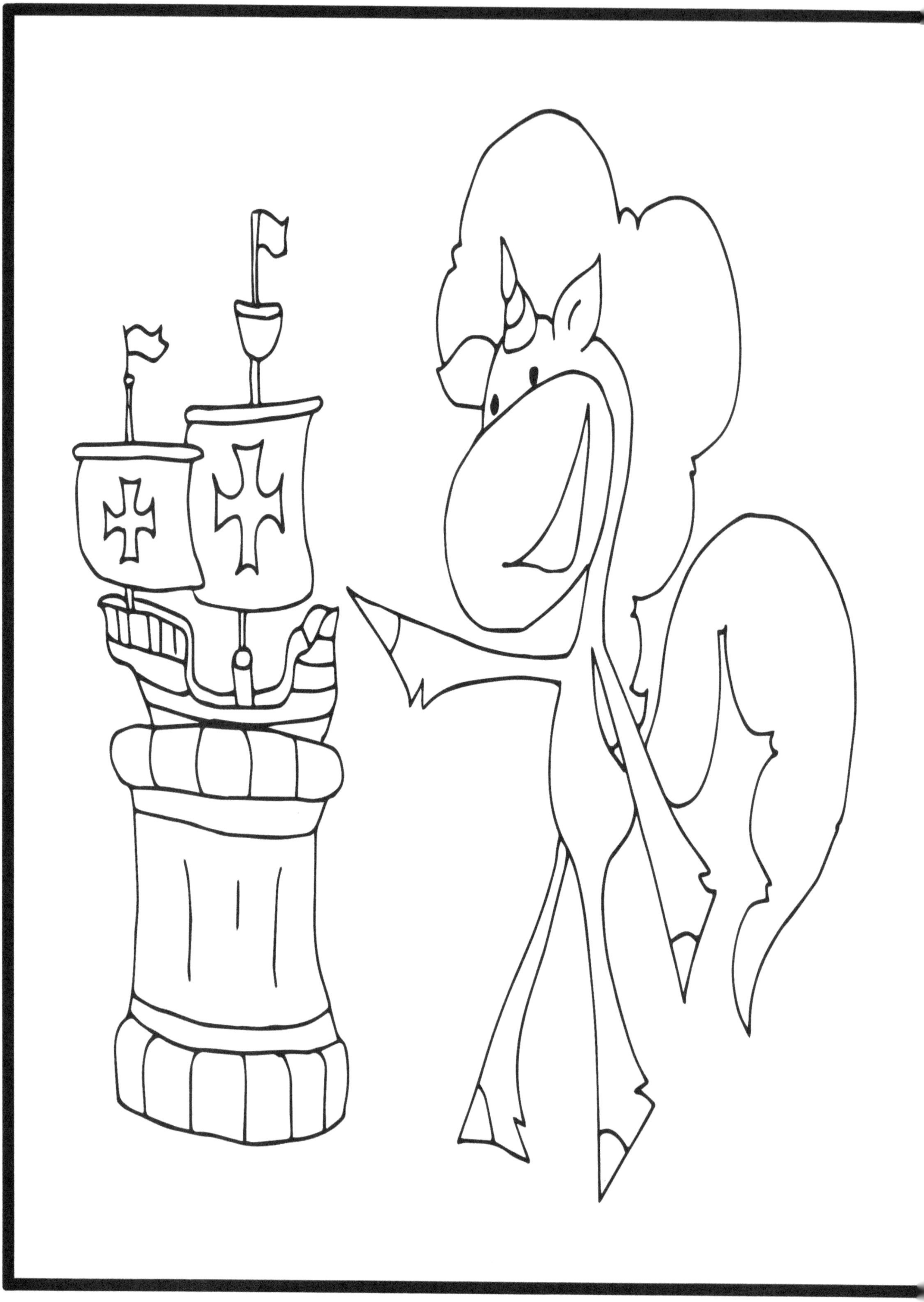

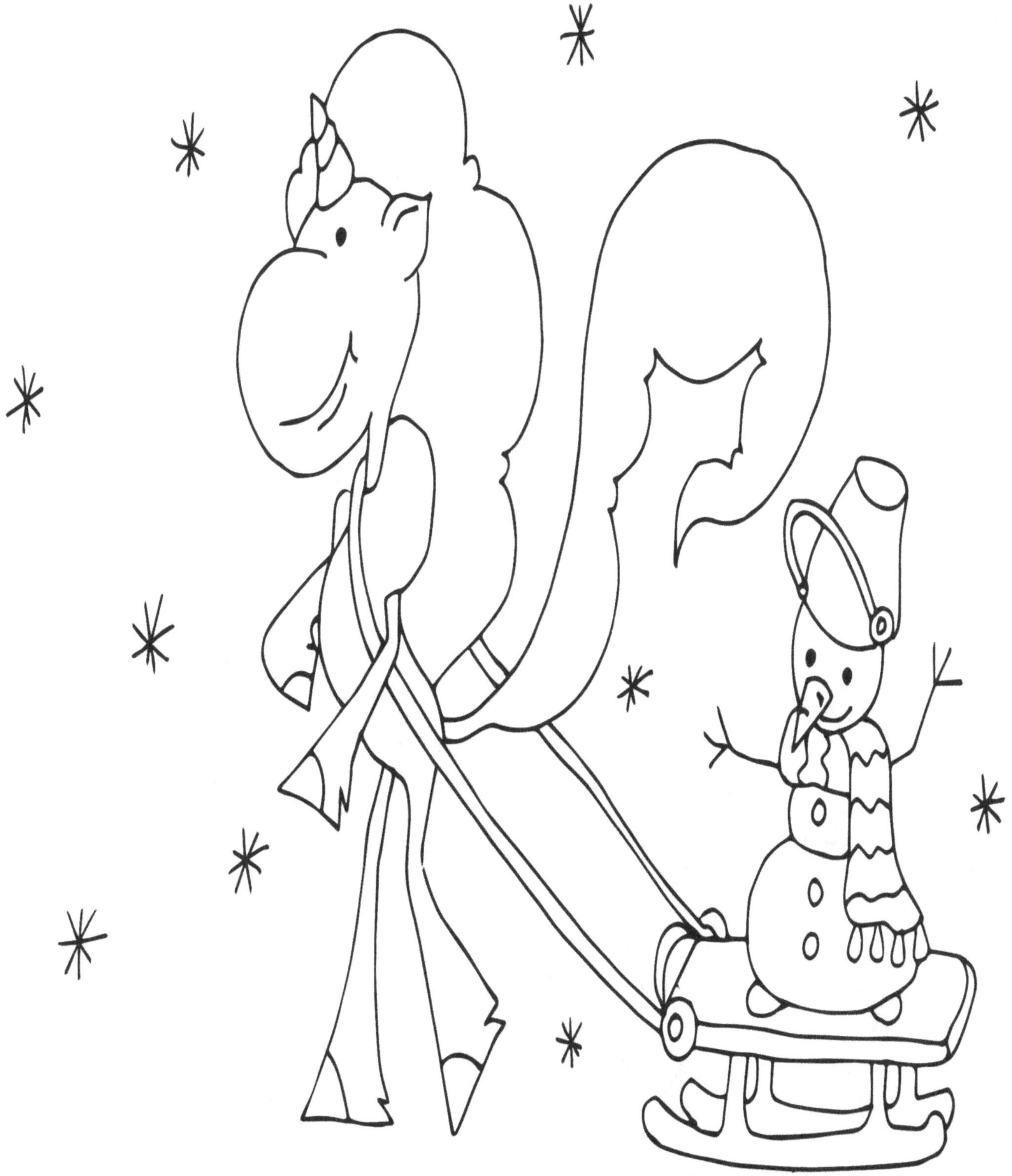

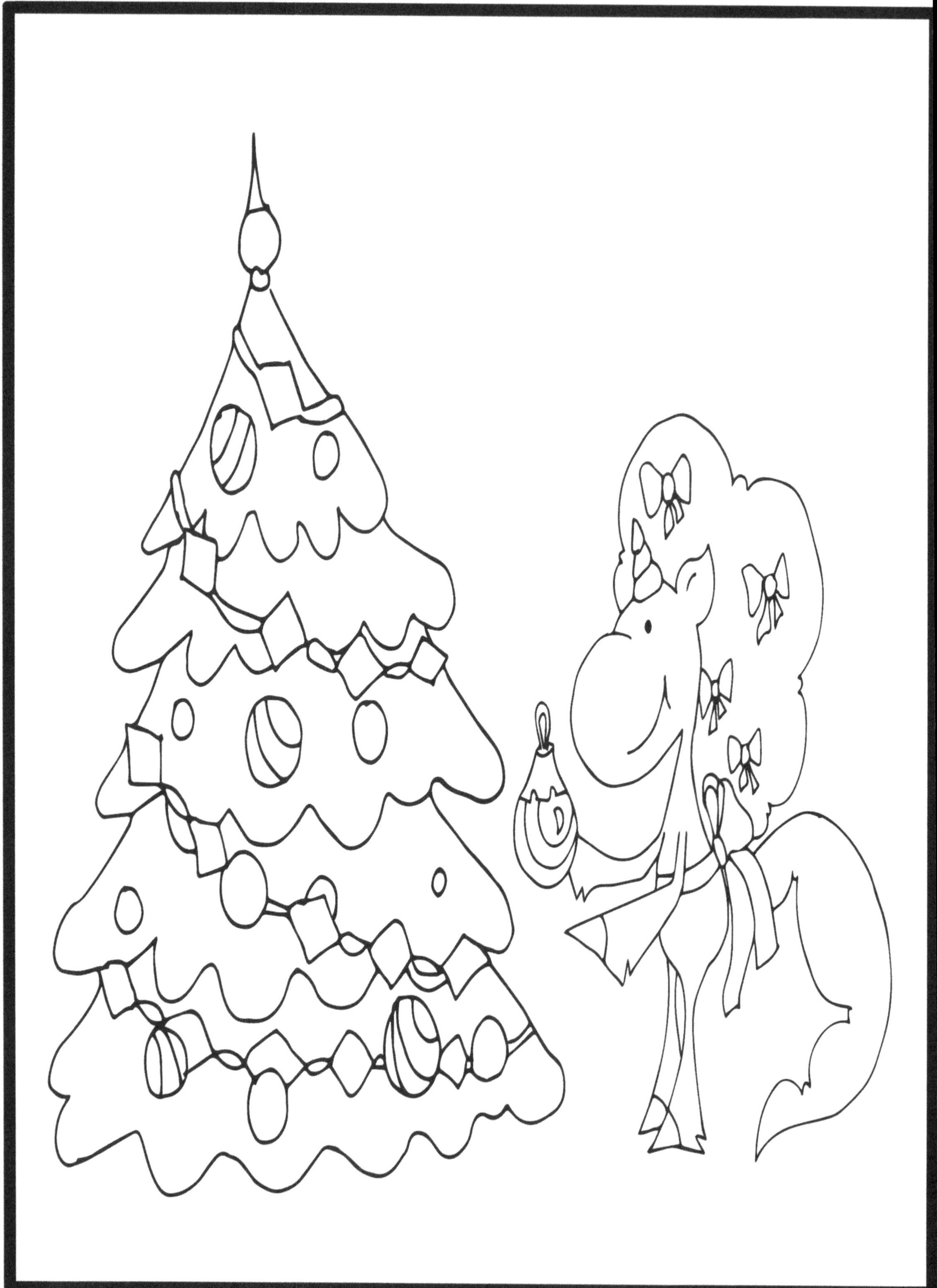

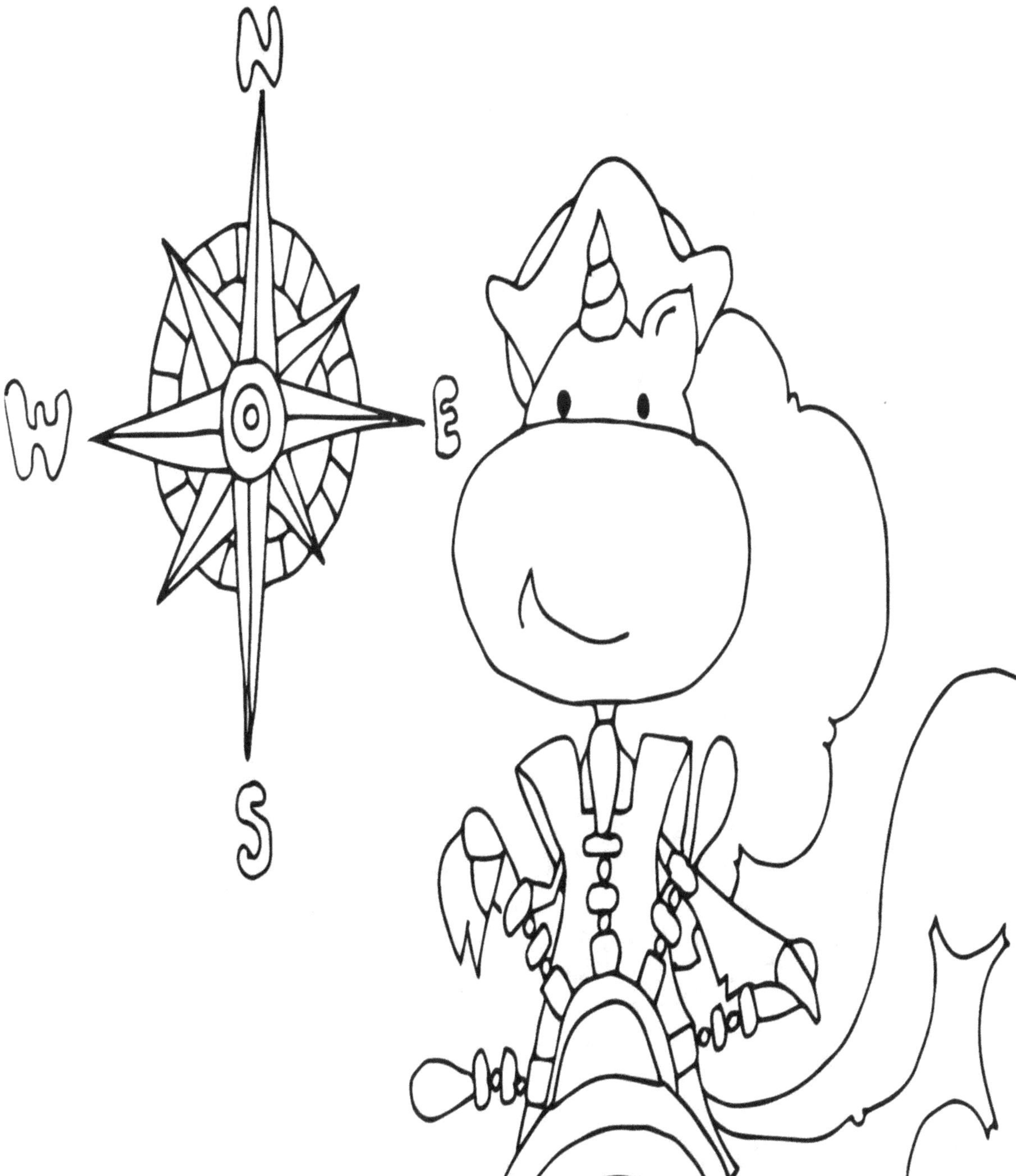
N
W
E
S

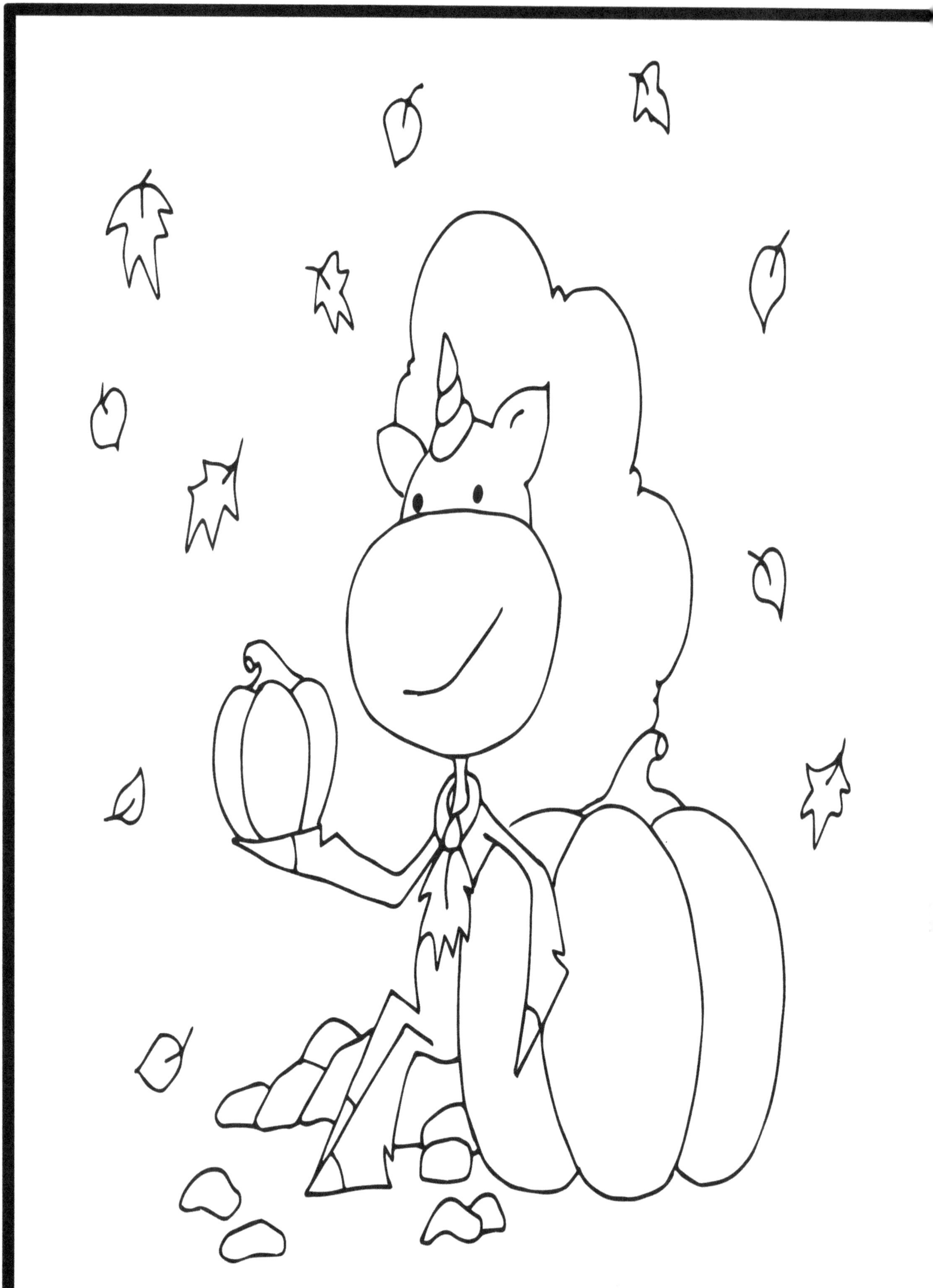

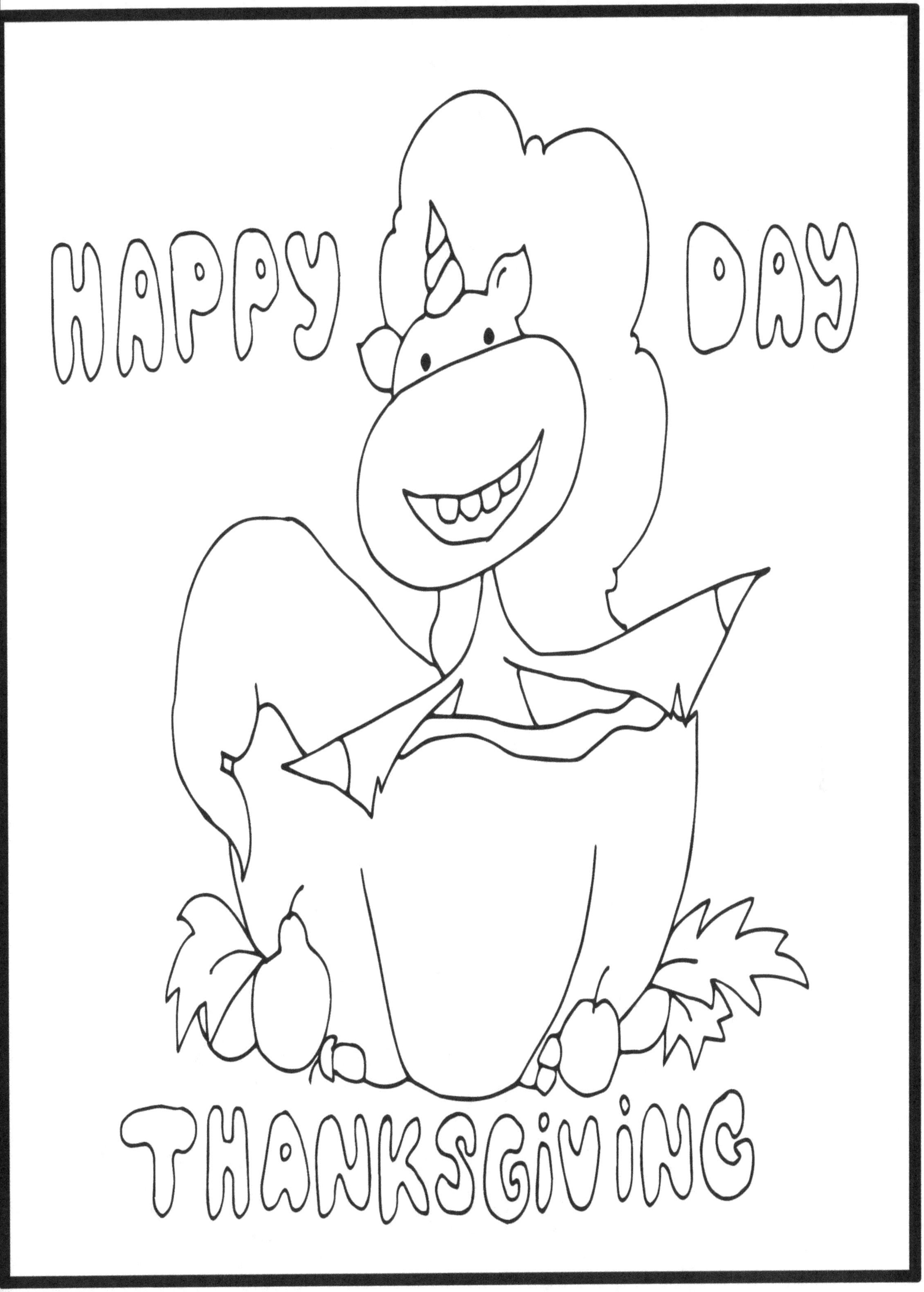
HAPPY
DAY
THANKSGIVING

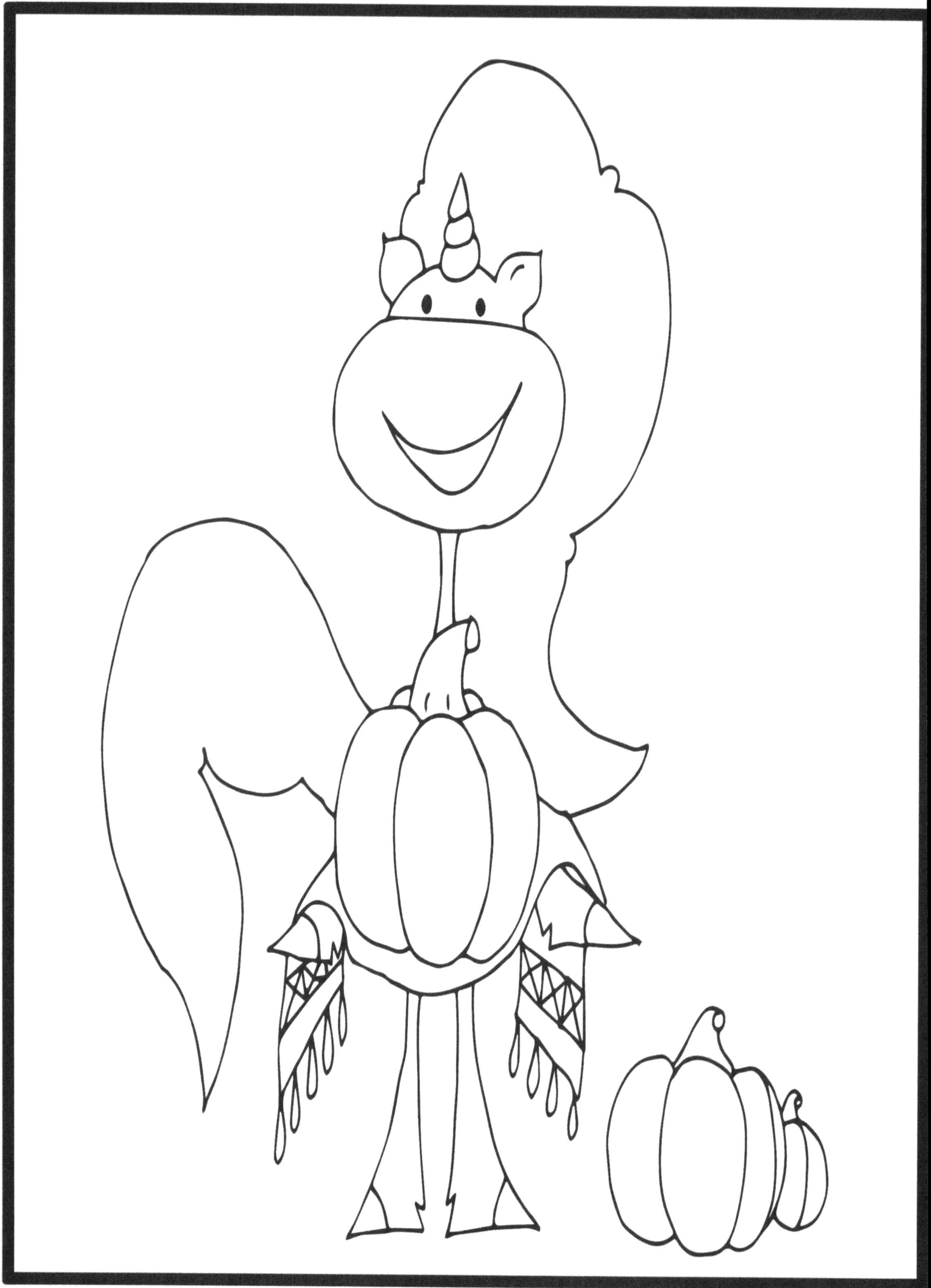

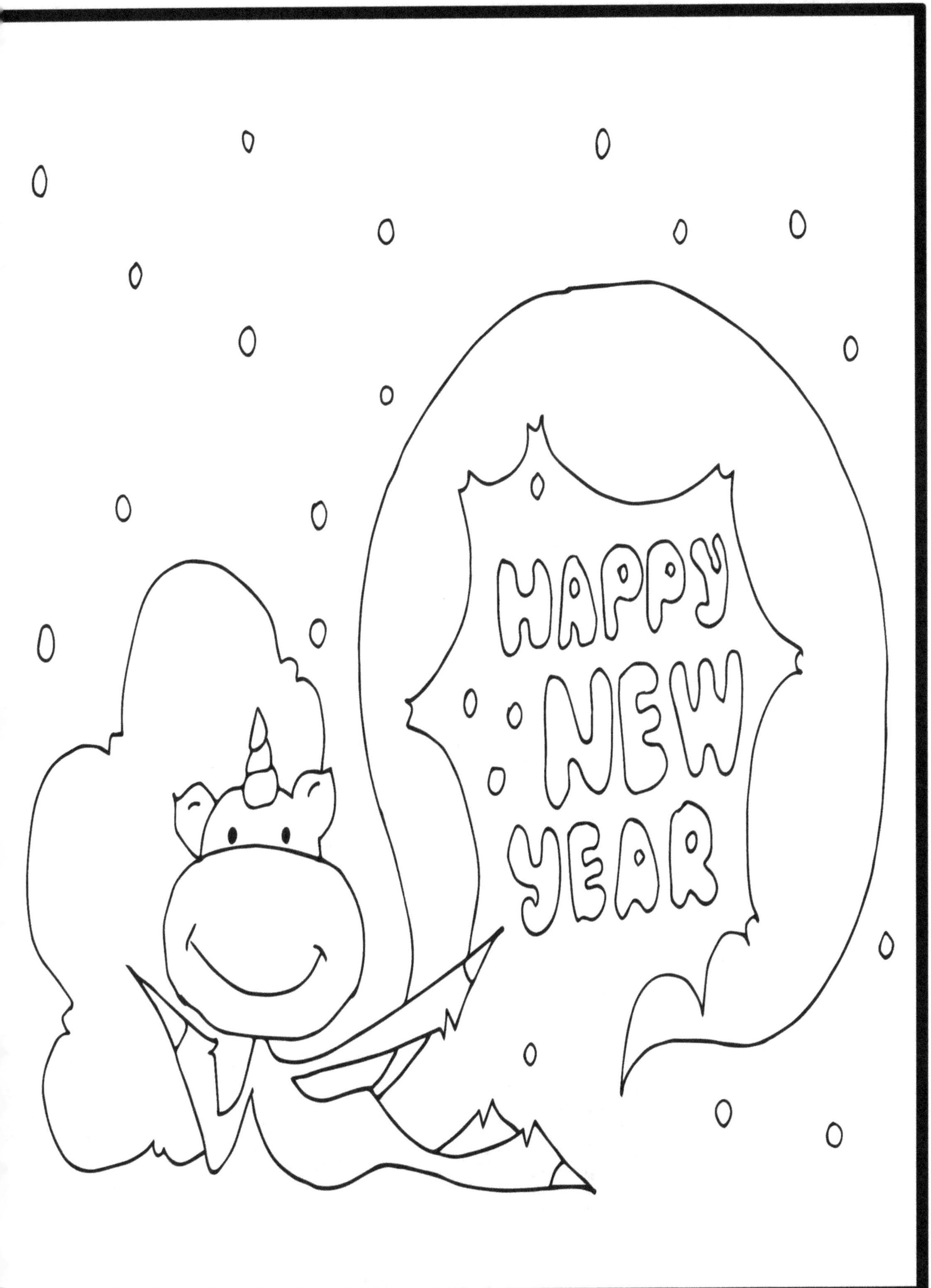
HAPPY
NEW
YEAR

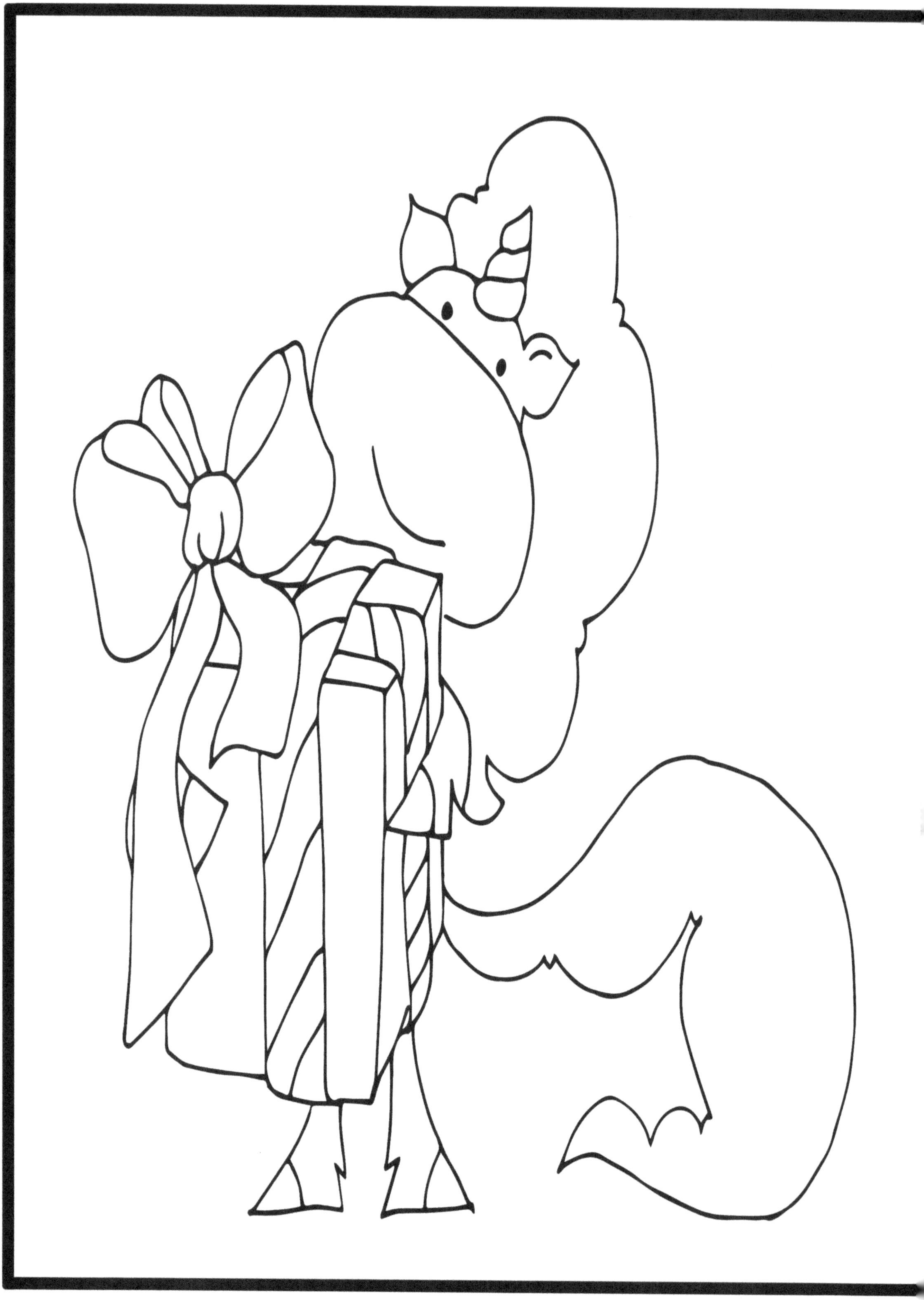

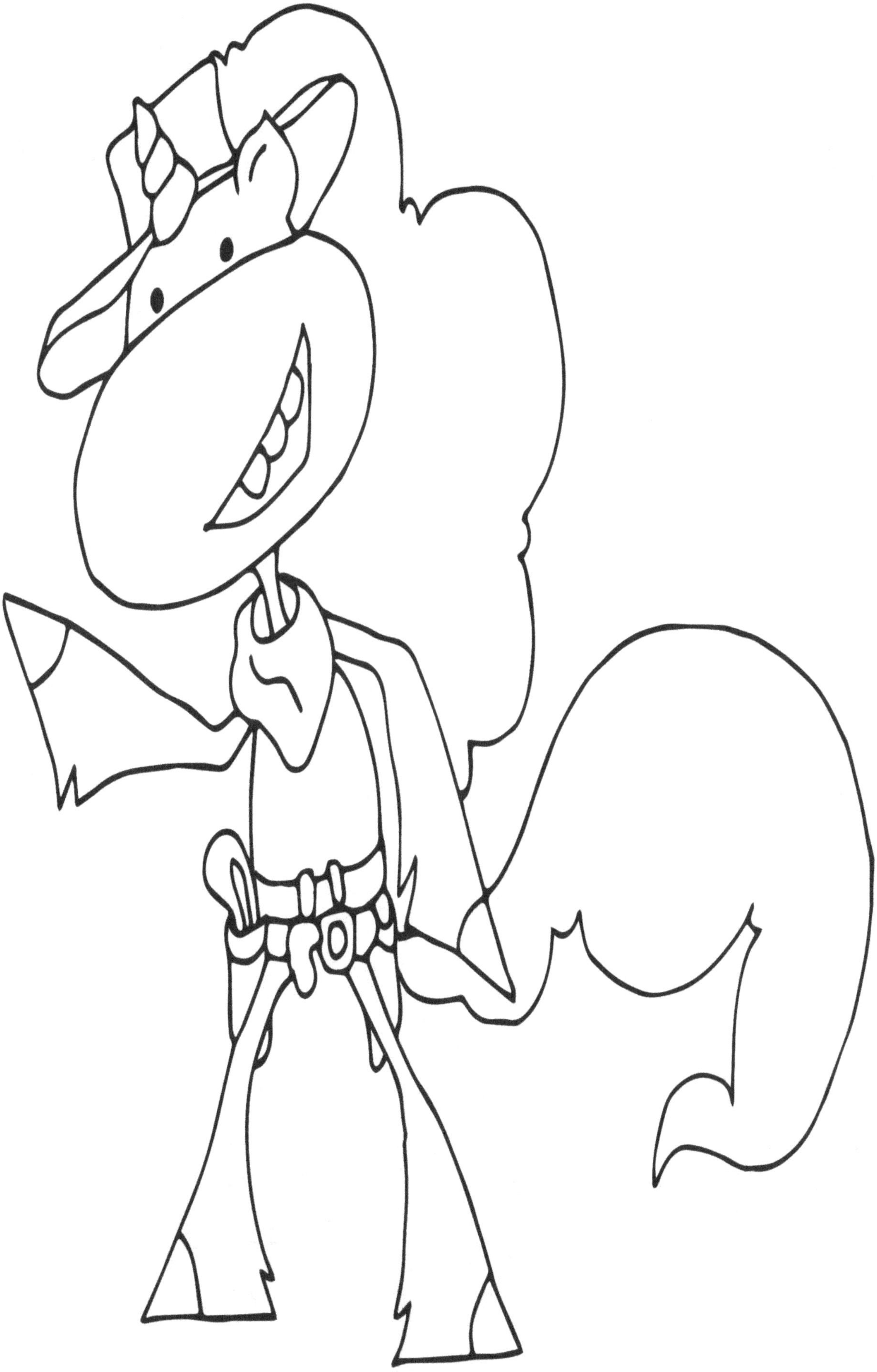

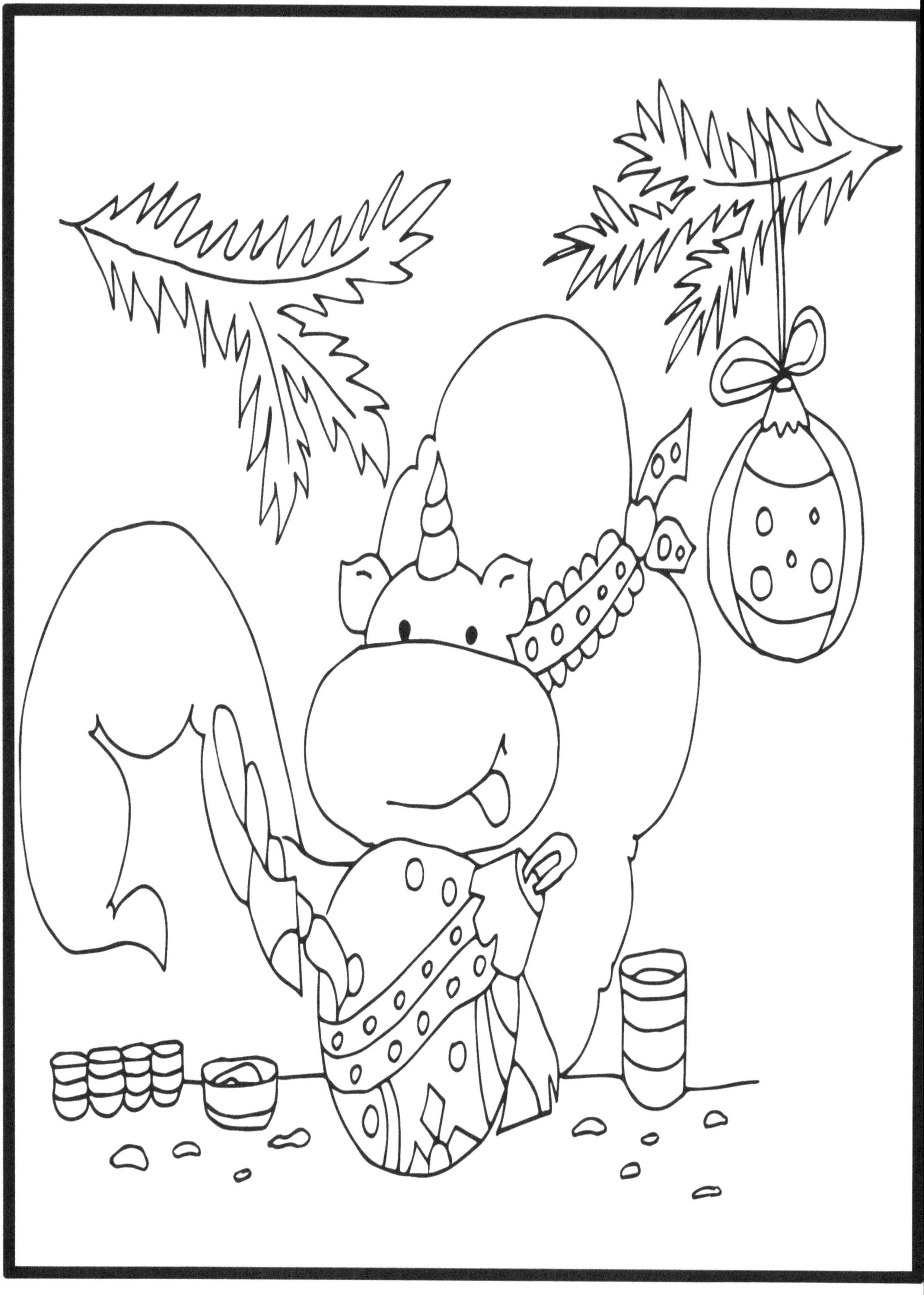

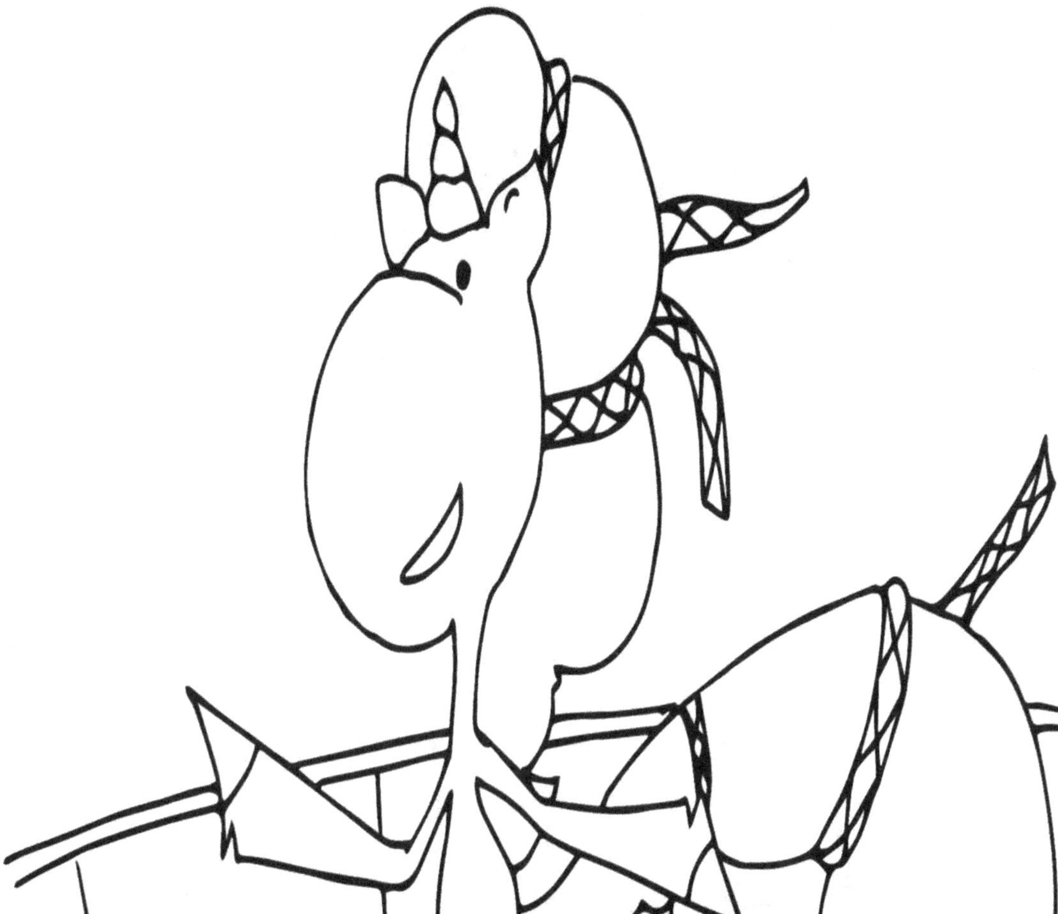

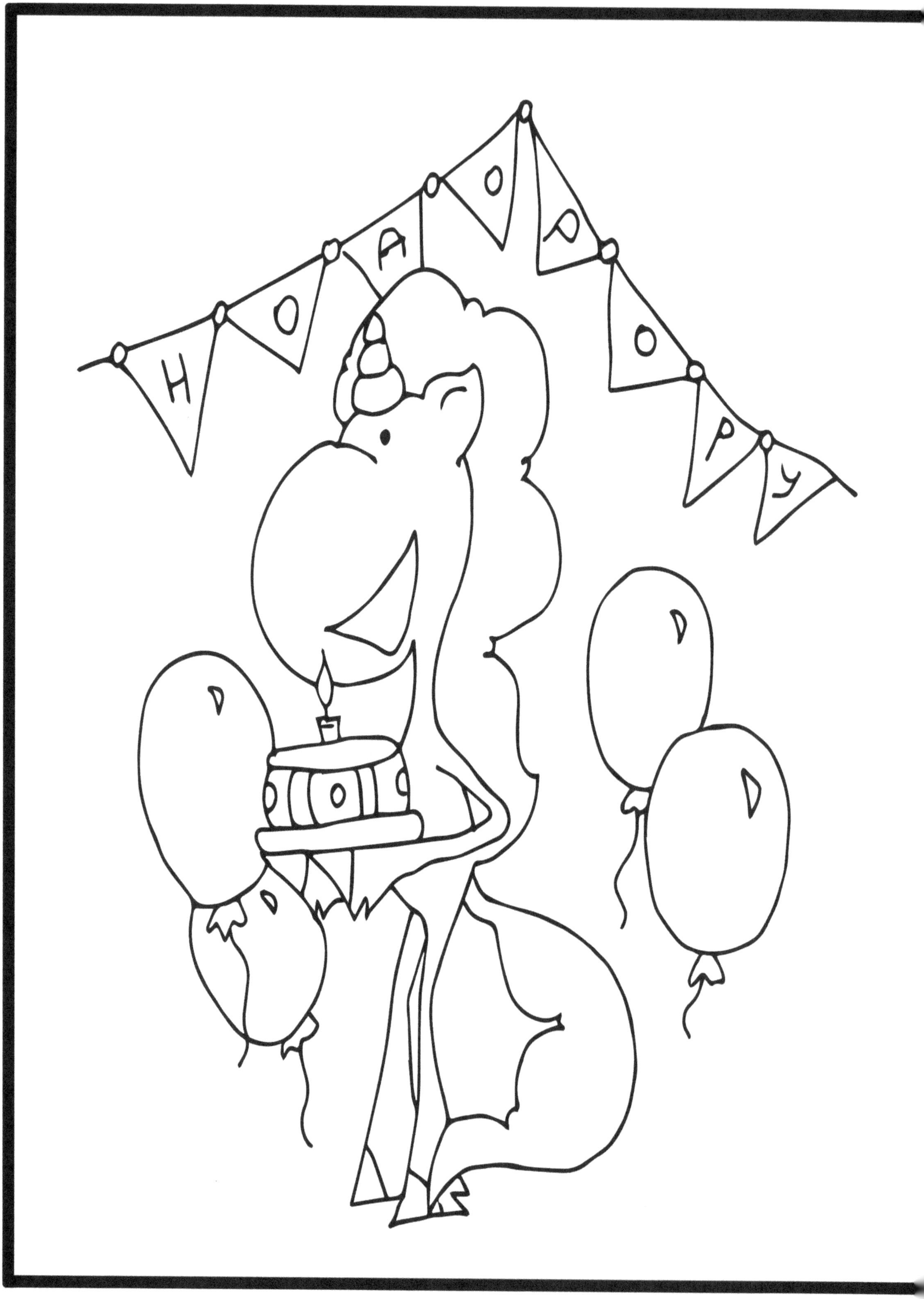

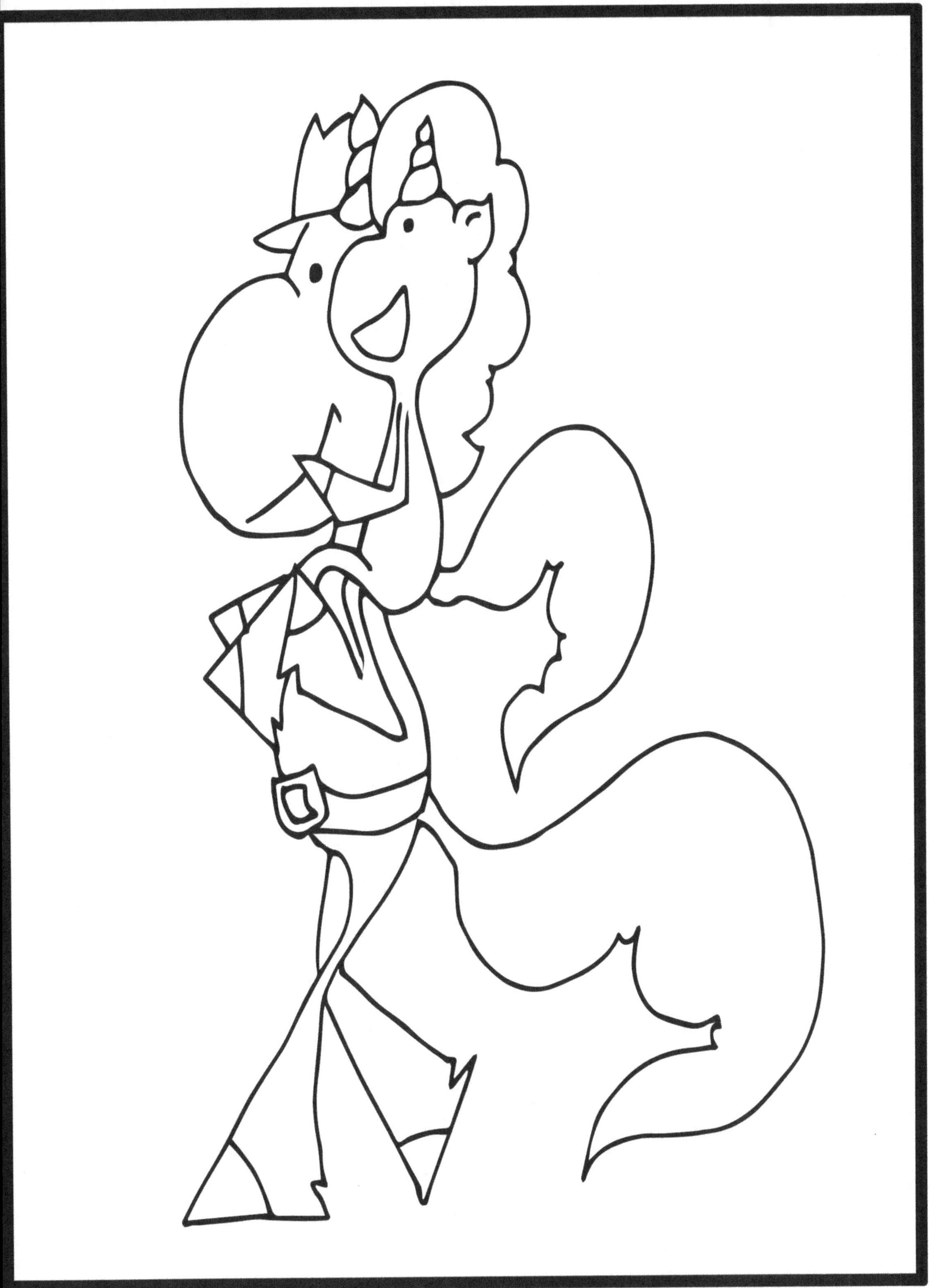

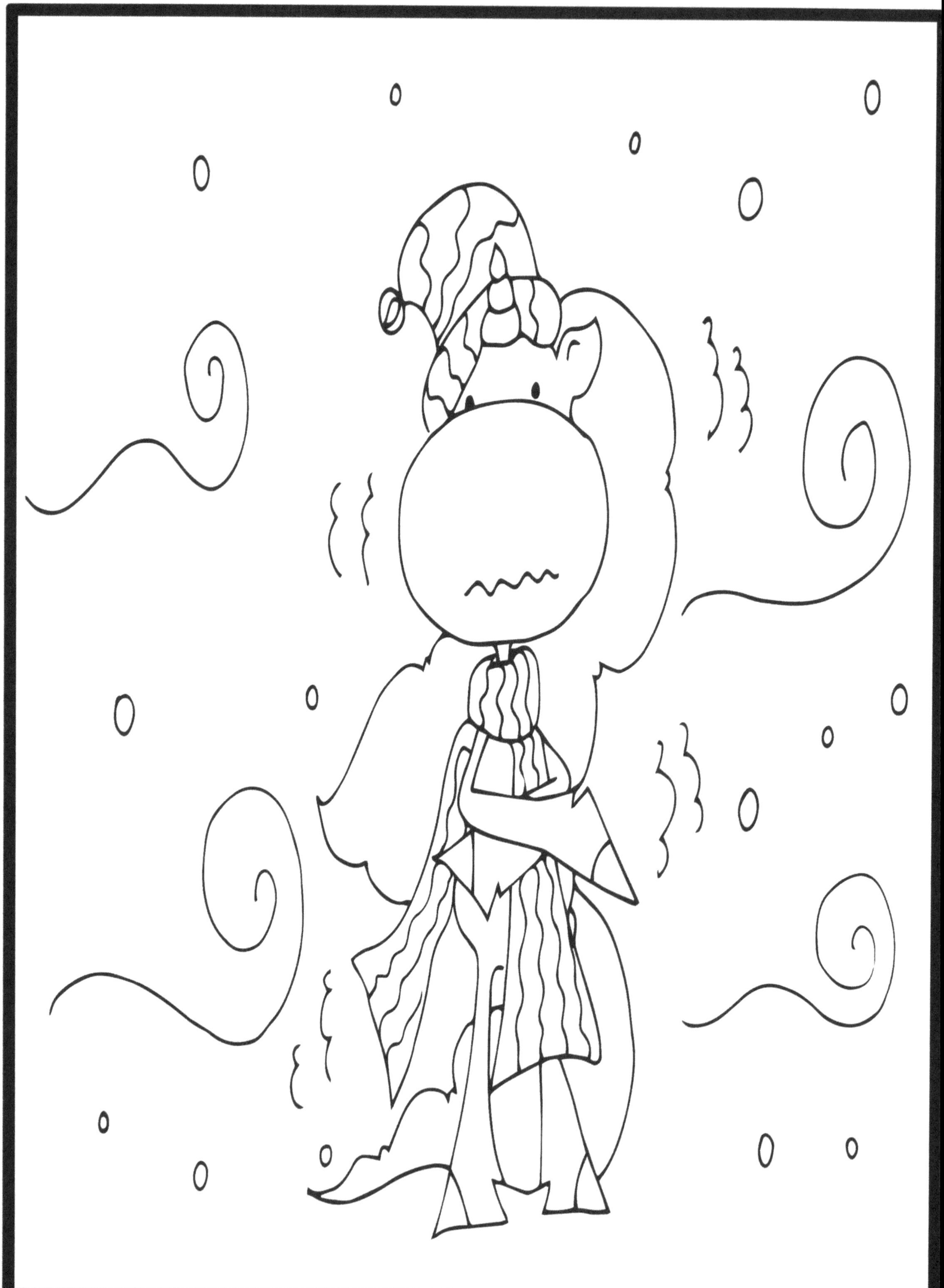

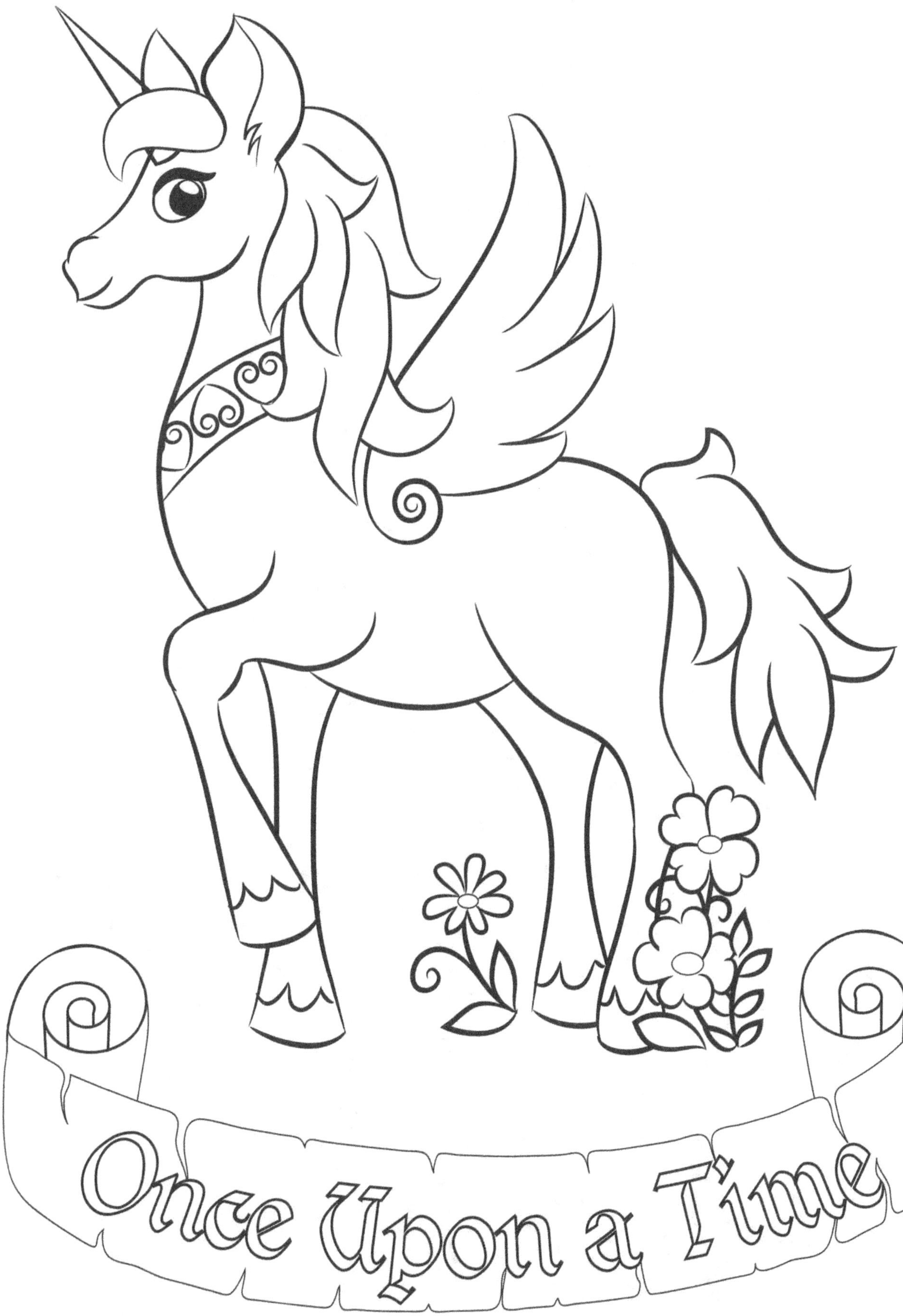
Once Upon a Time

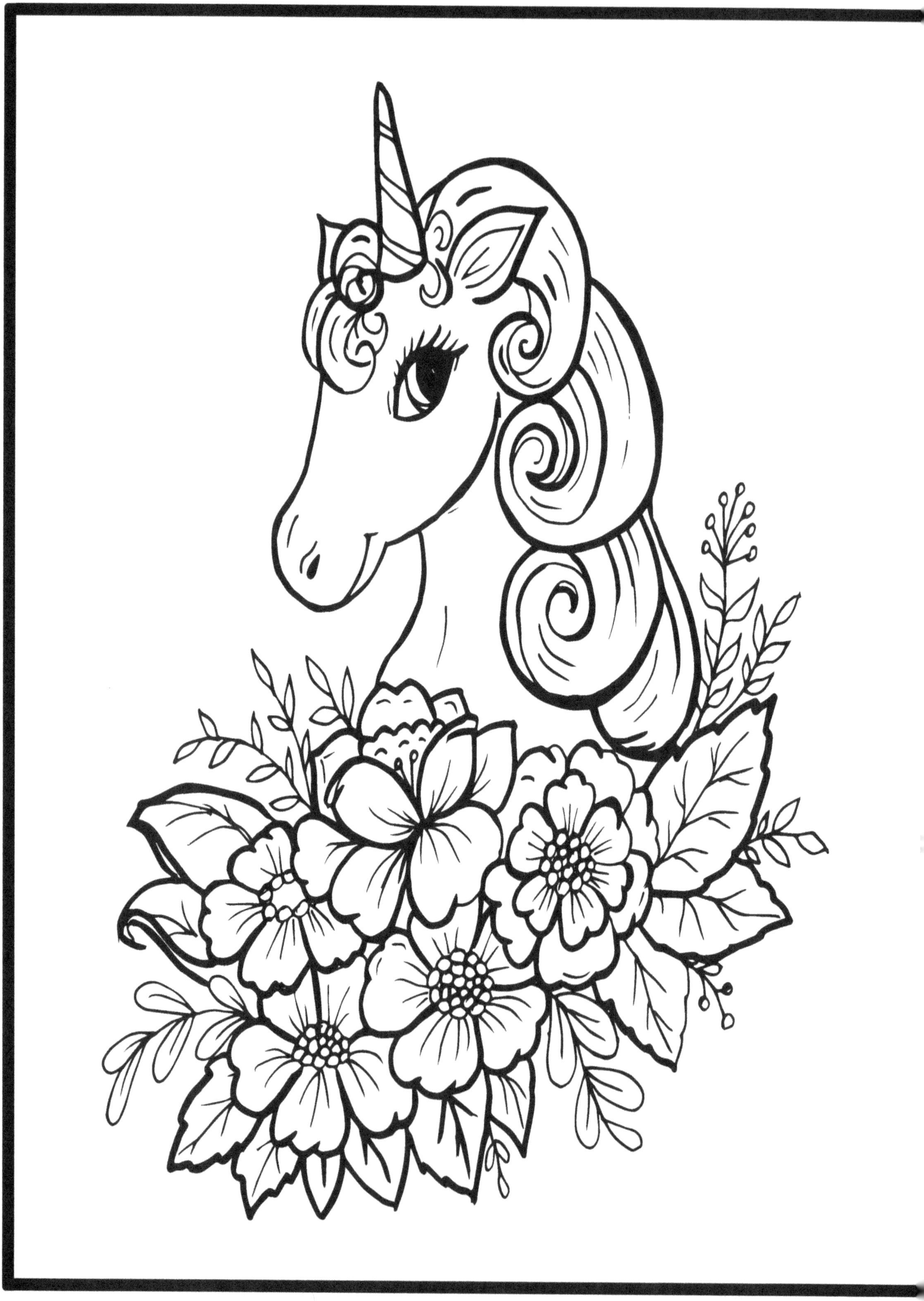

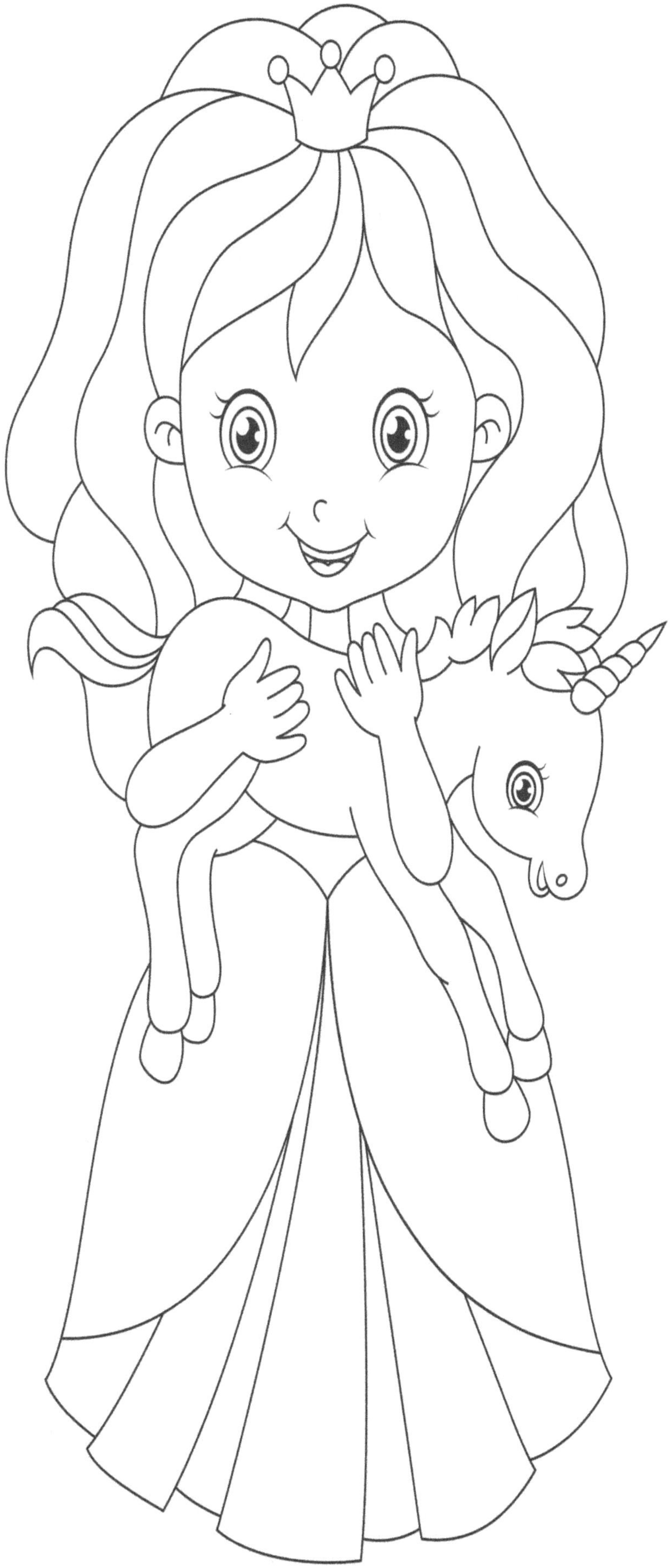

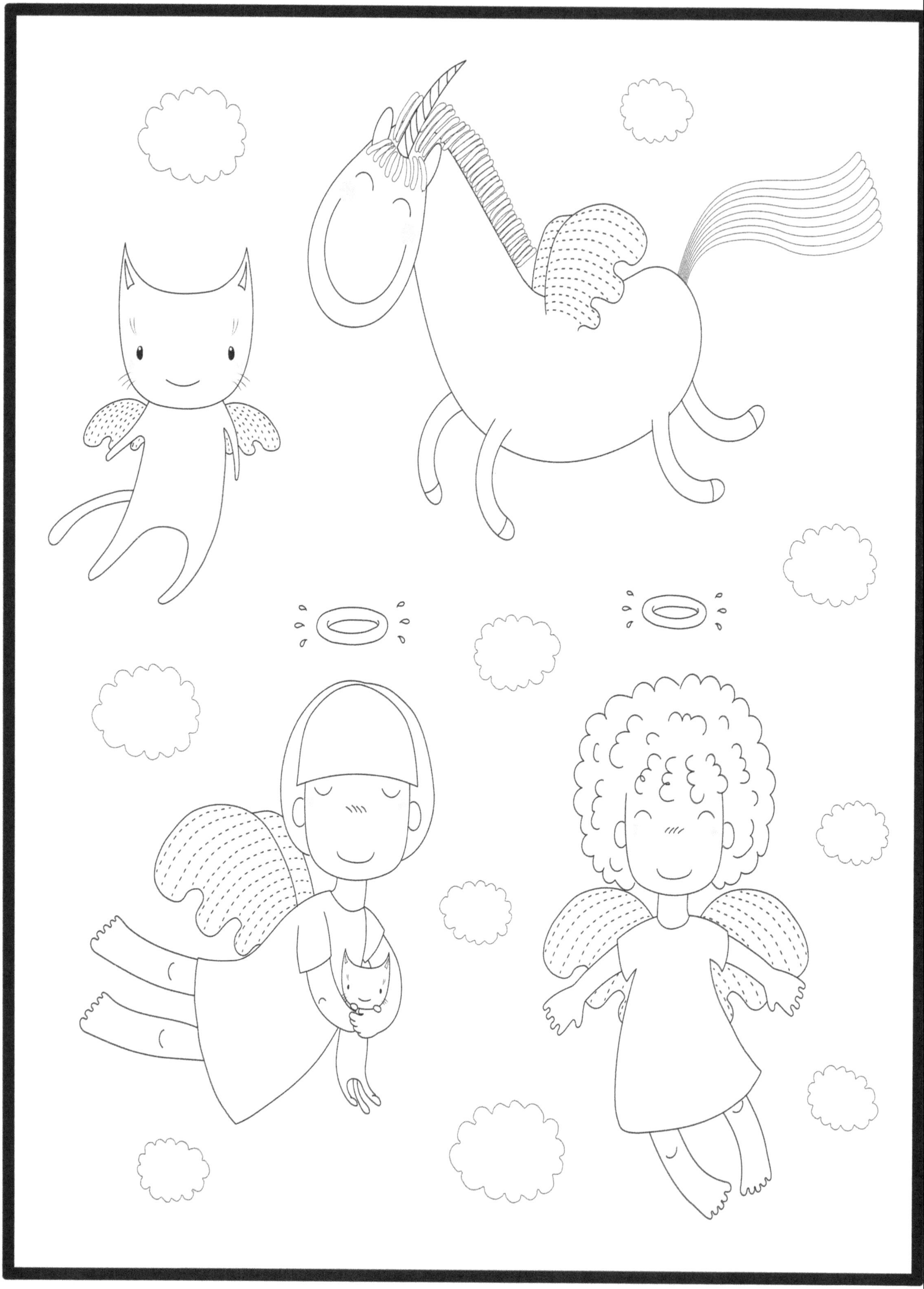

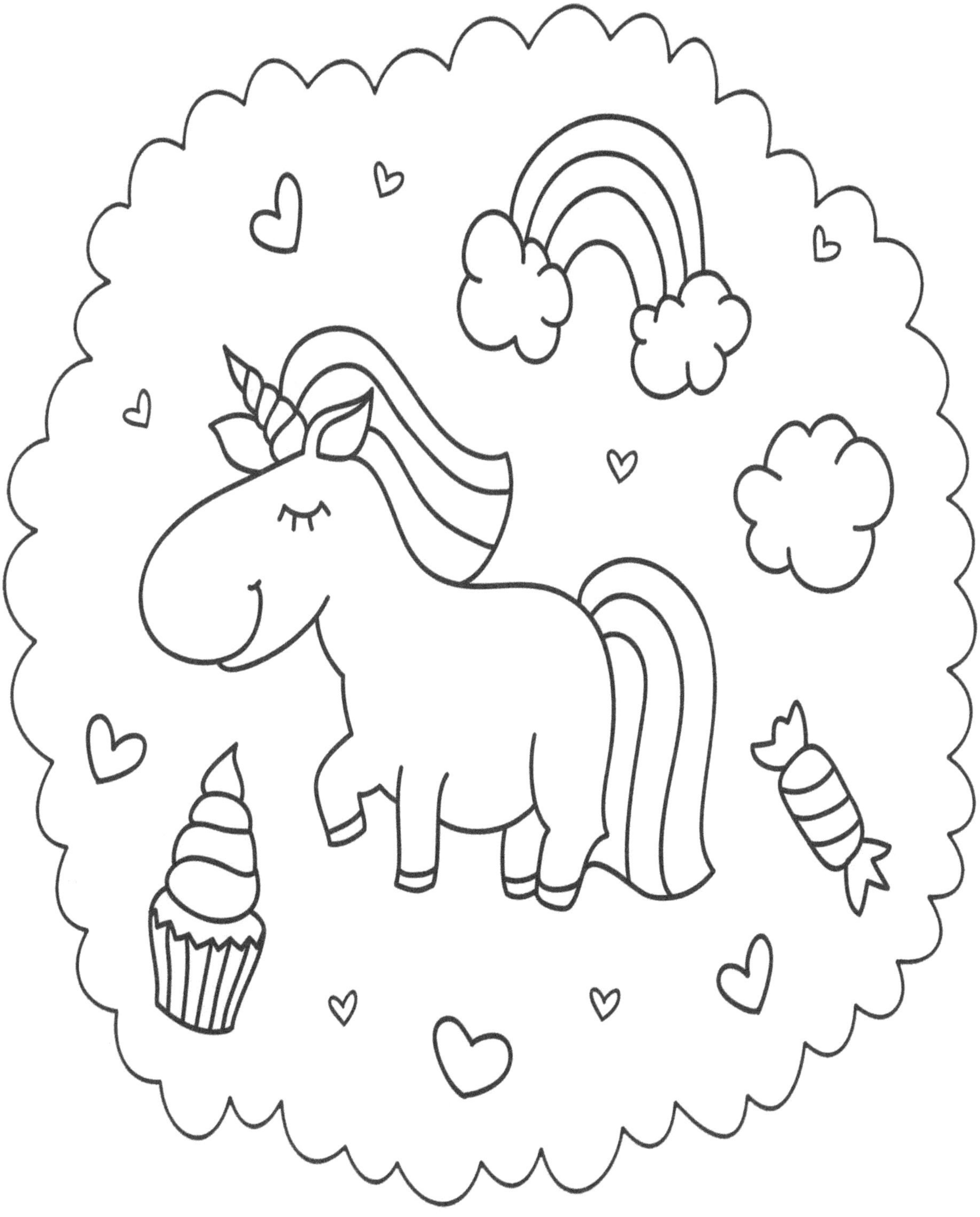

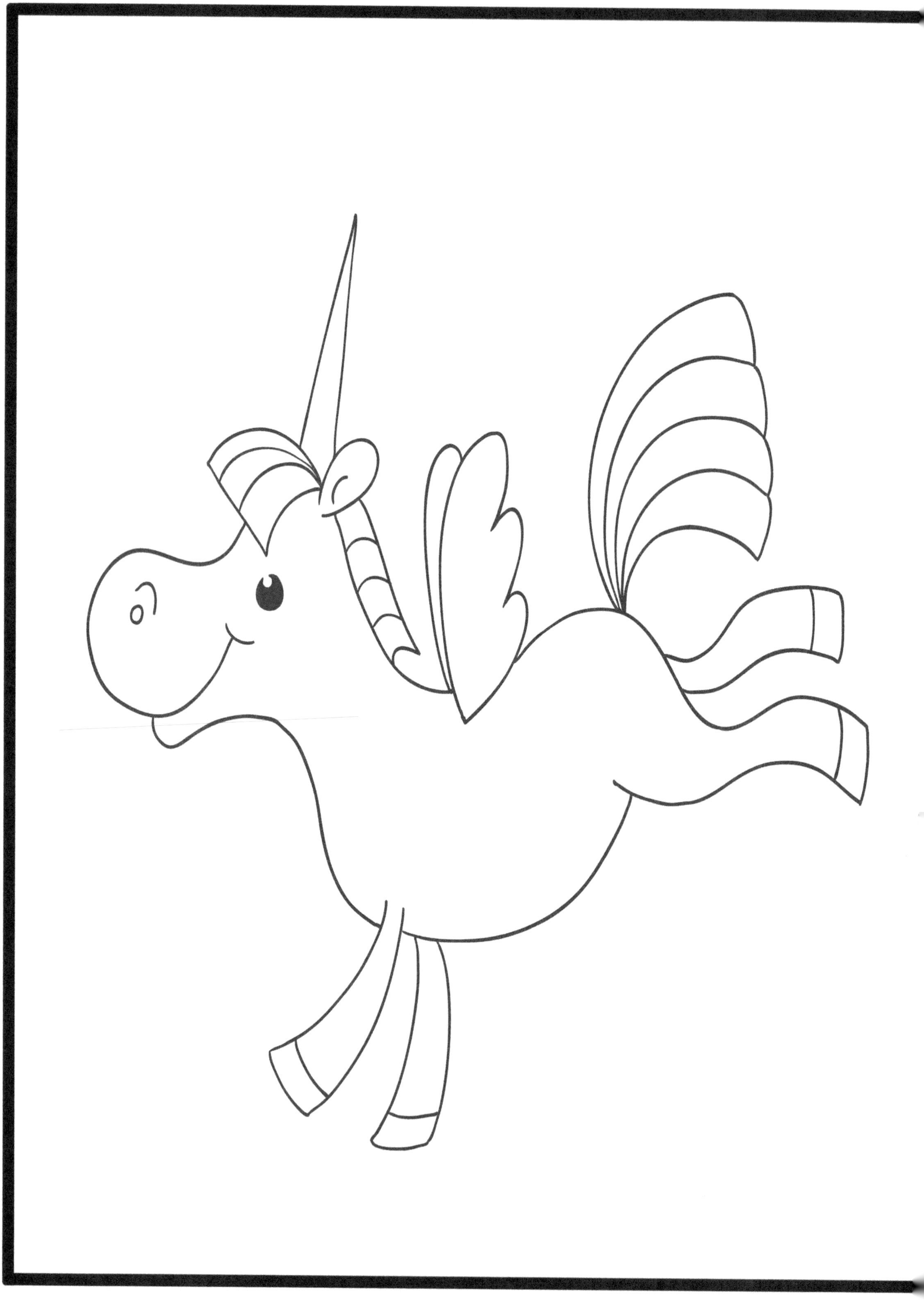

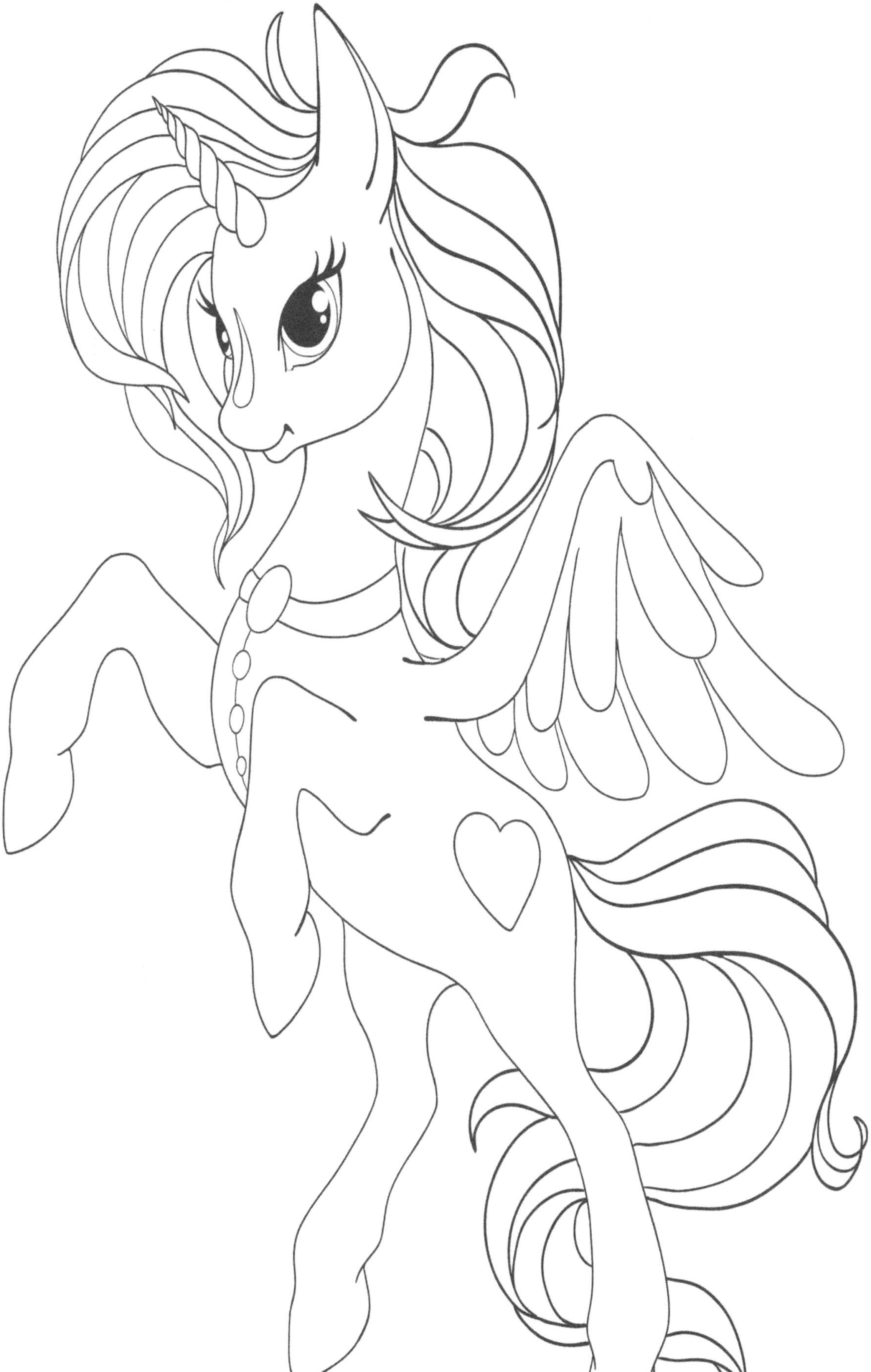

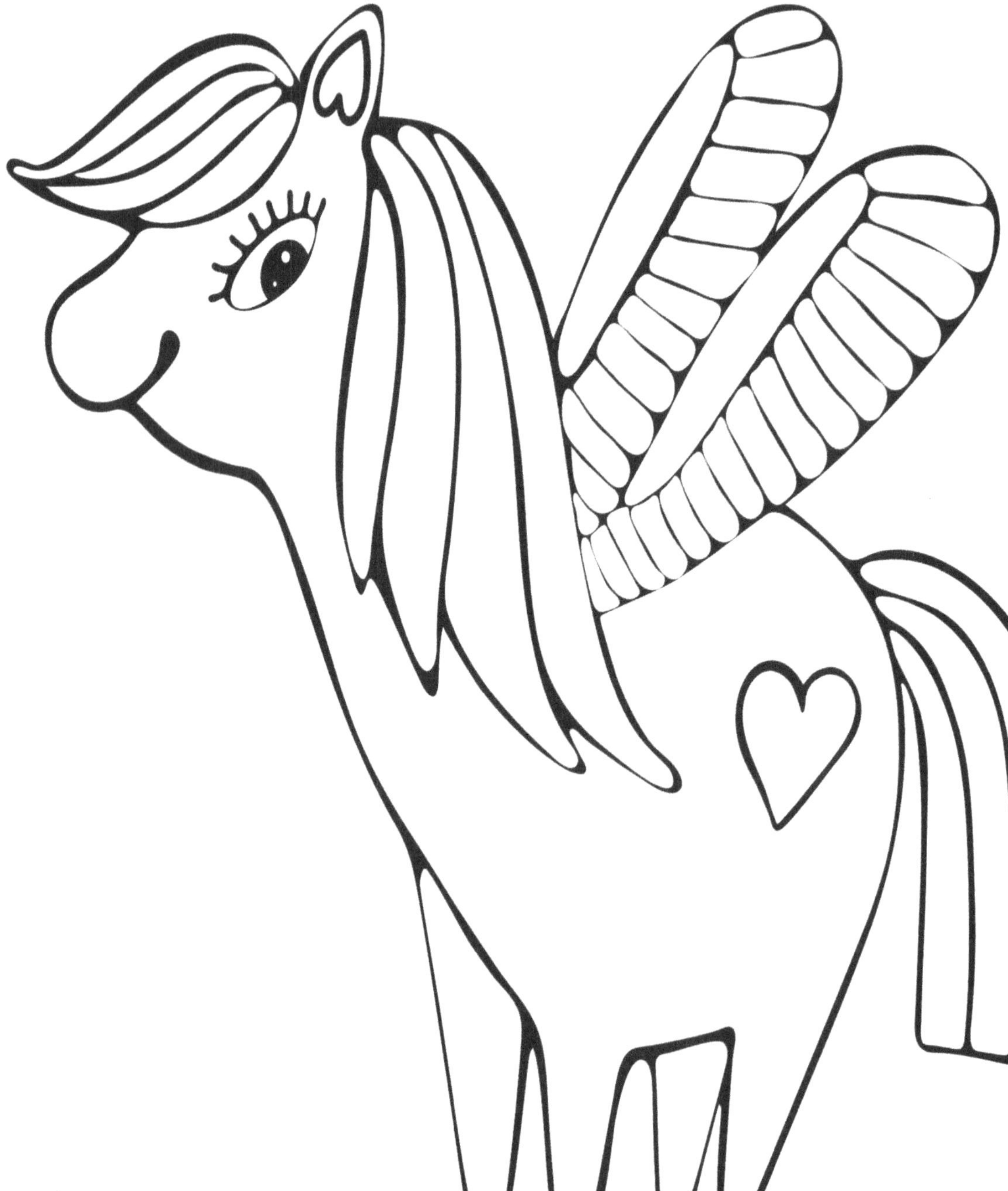

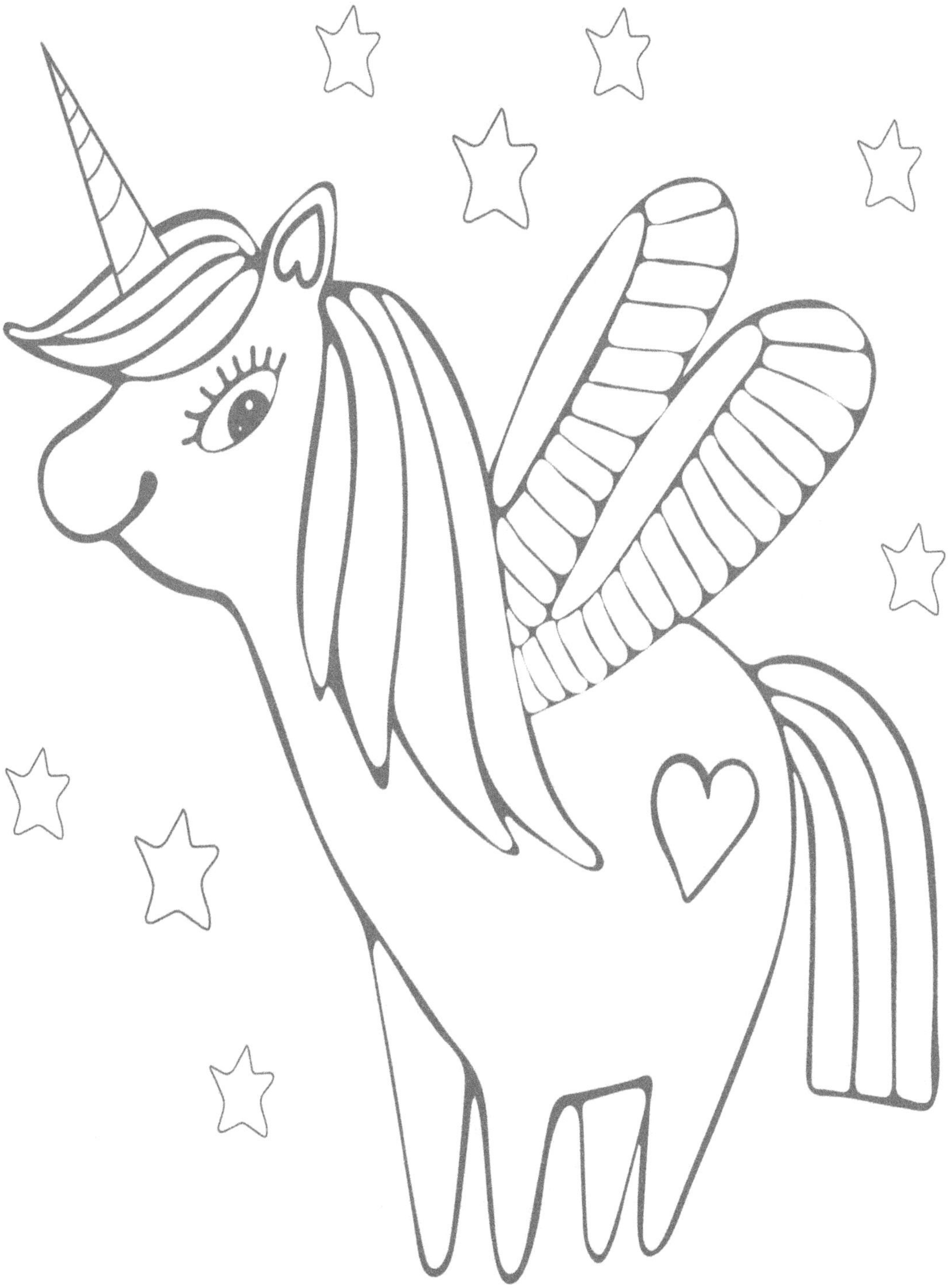

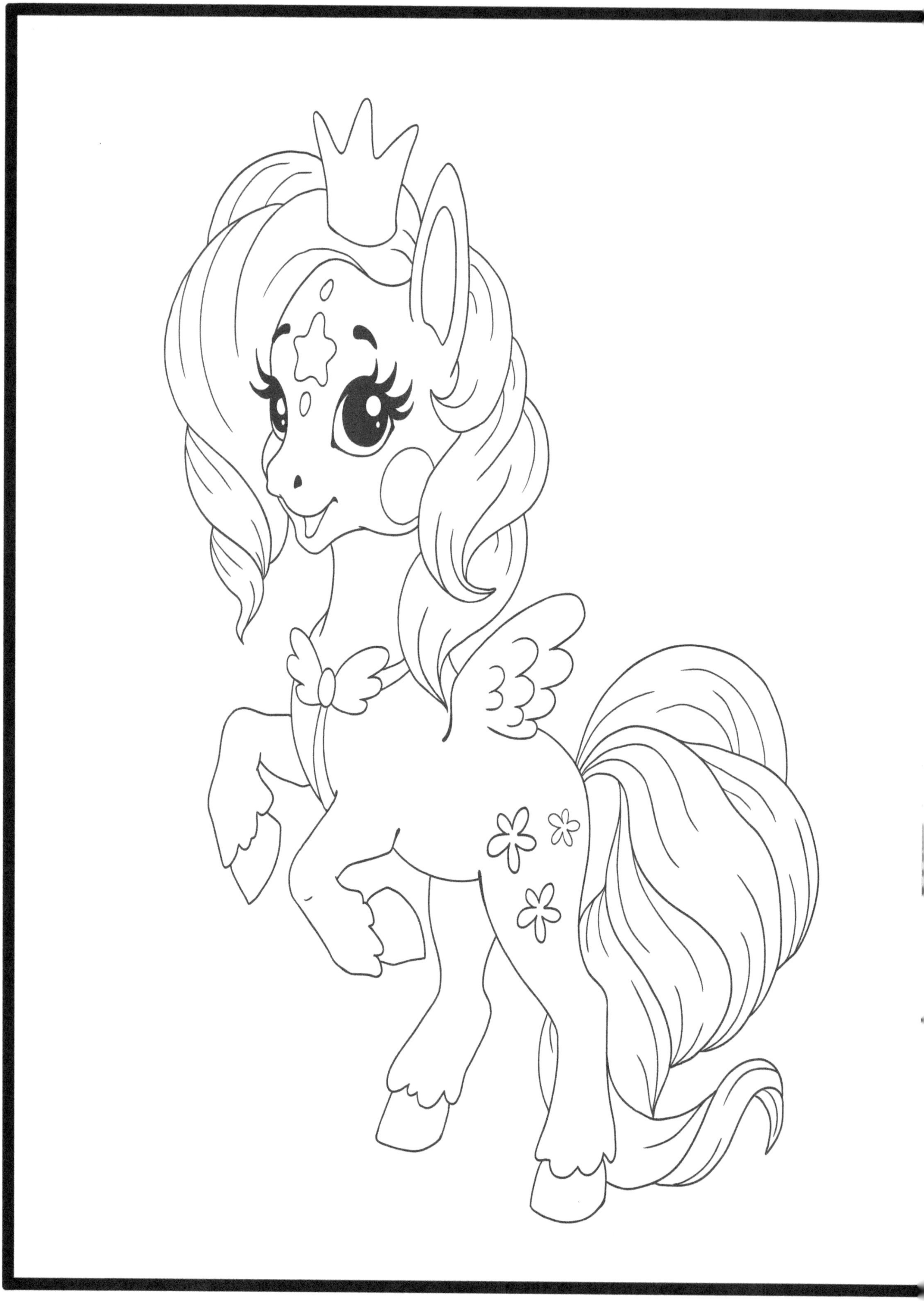

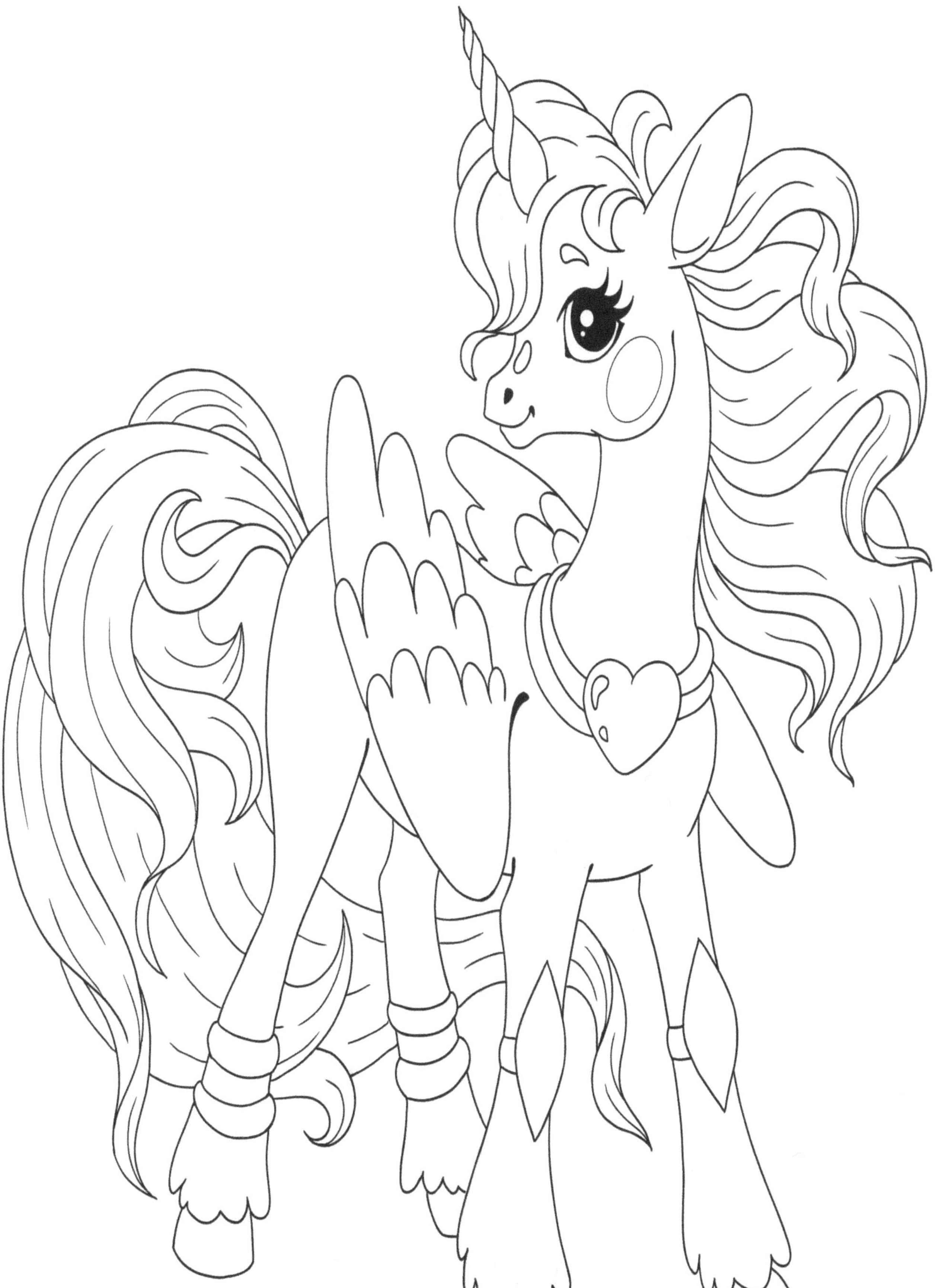

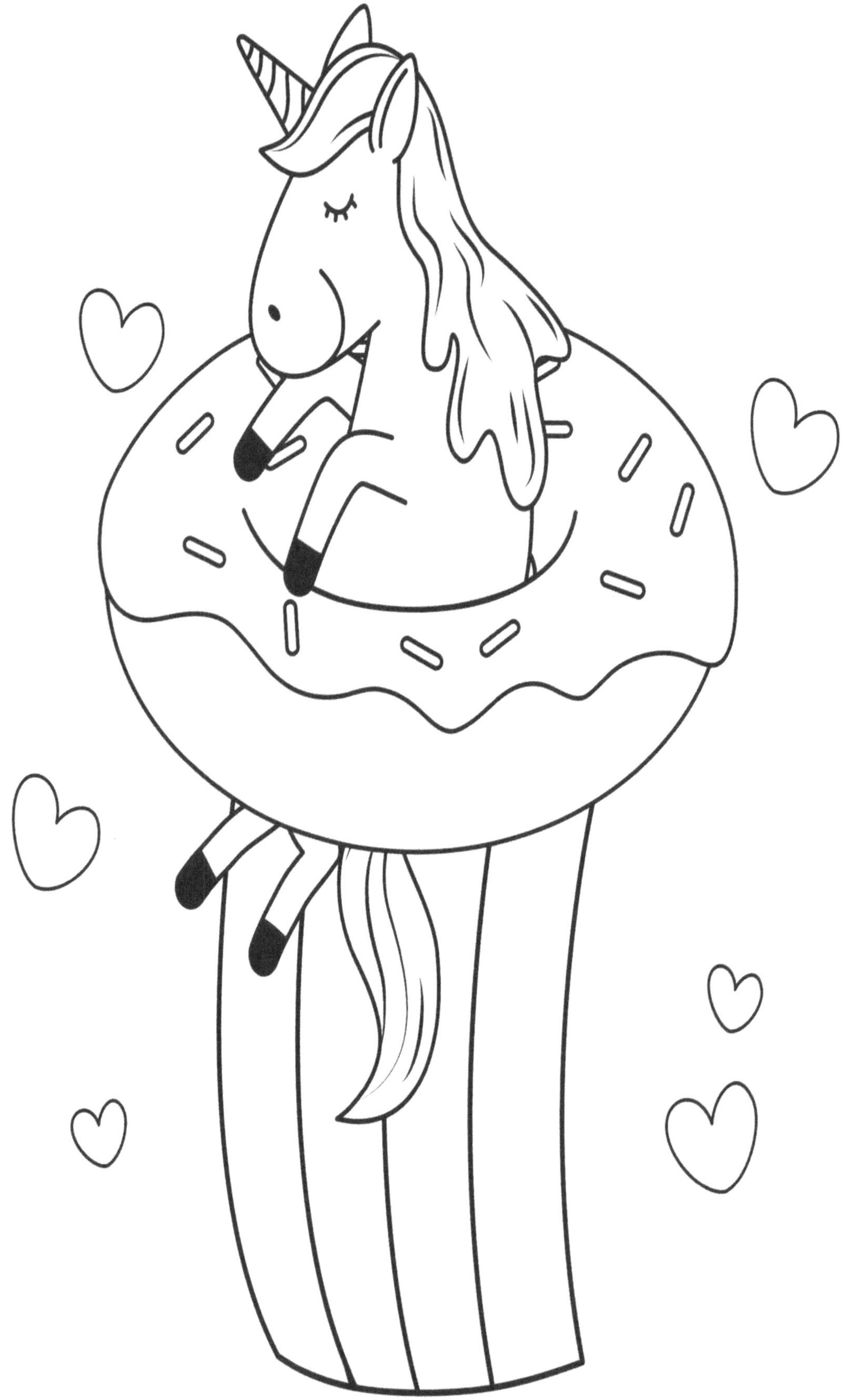

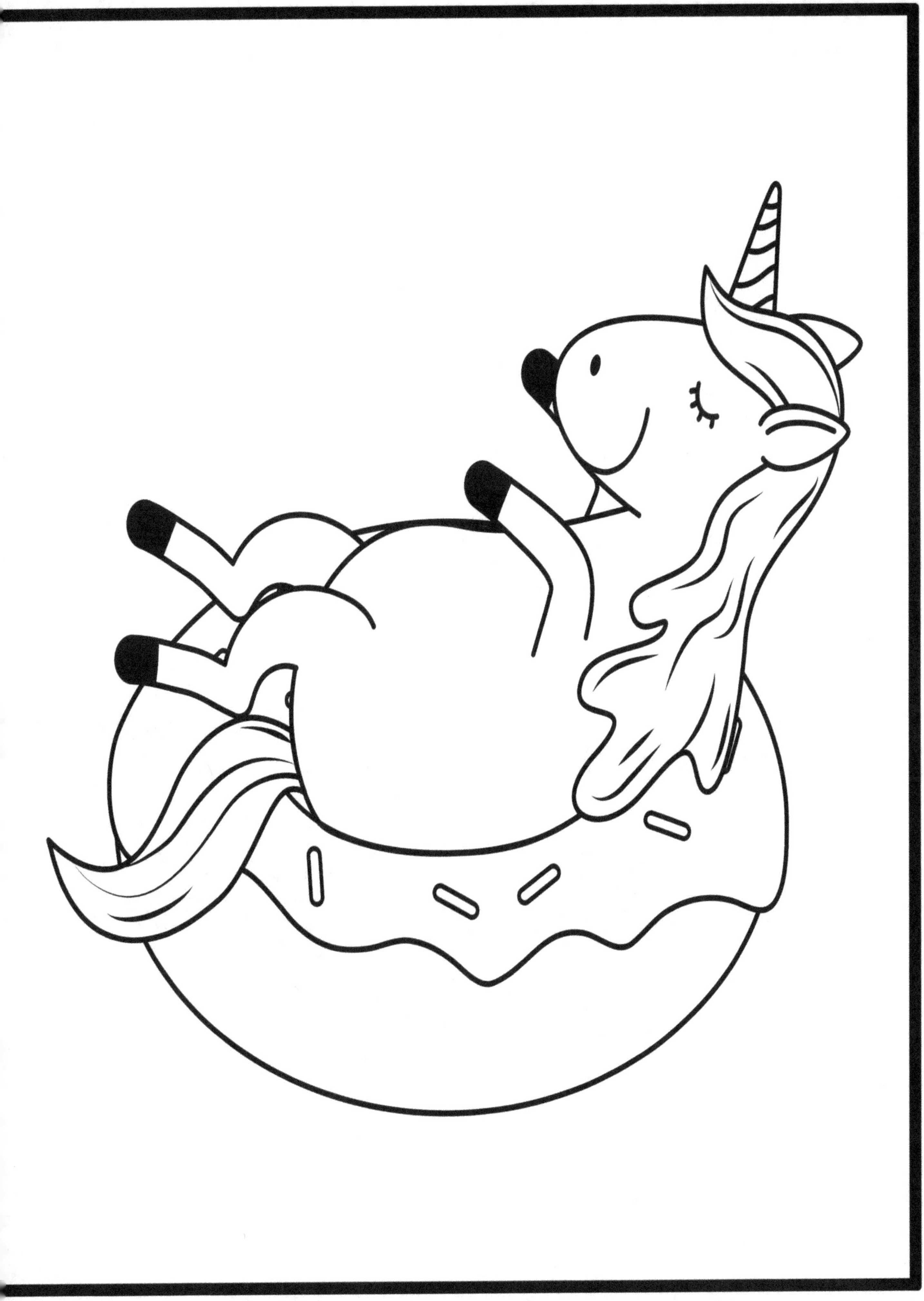

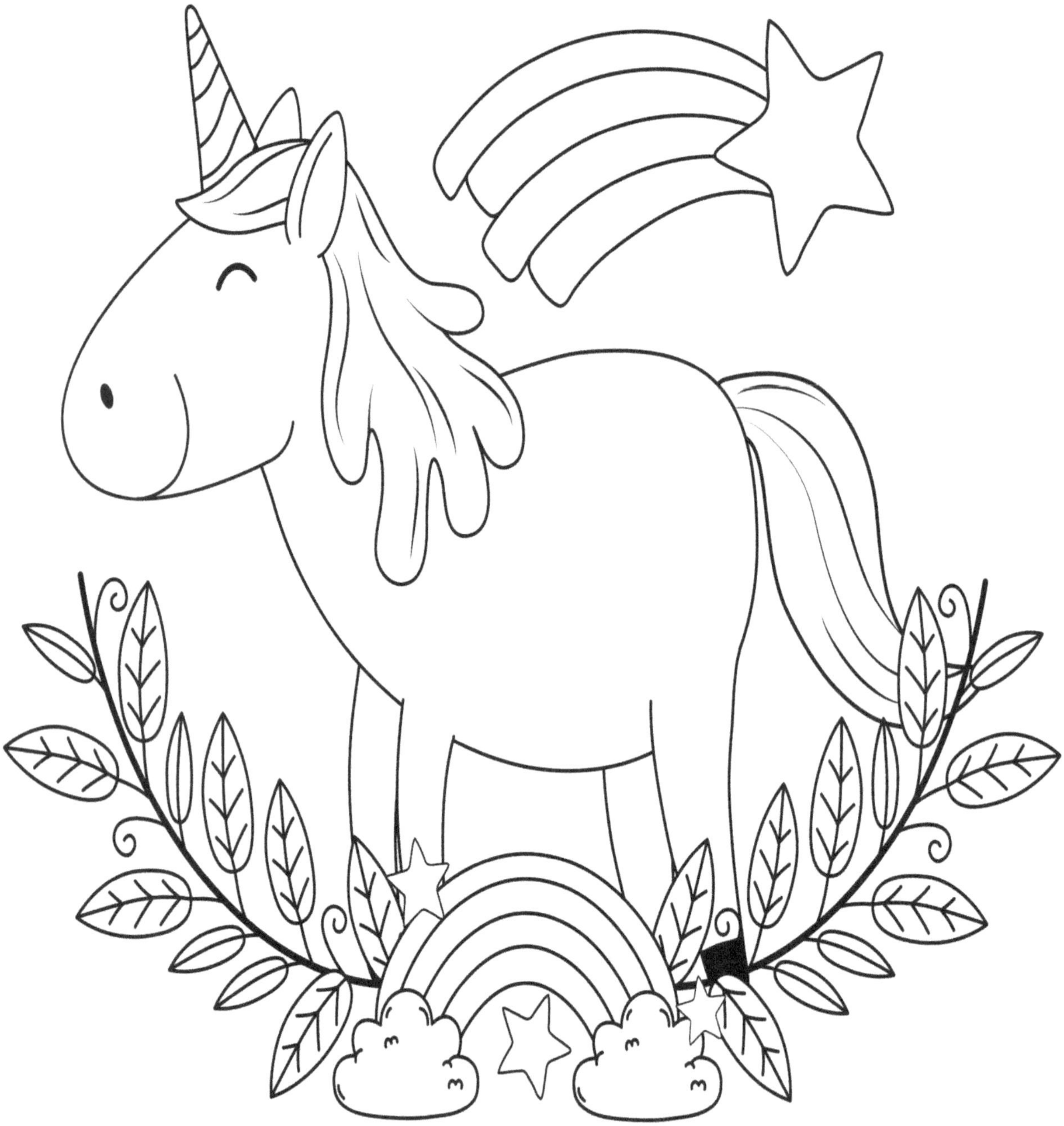

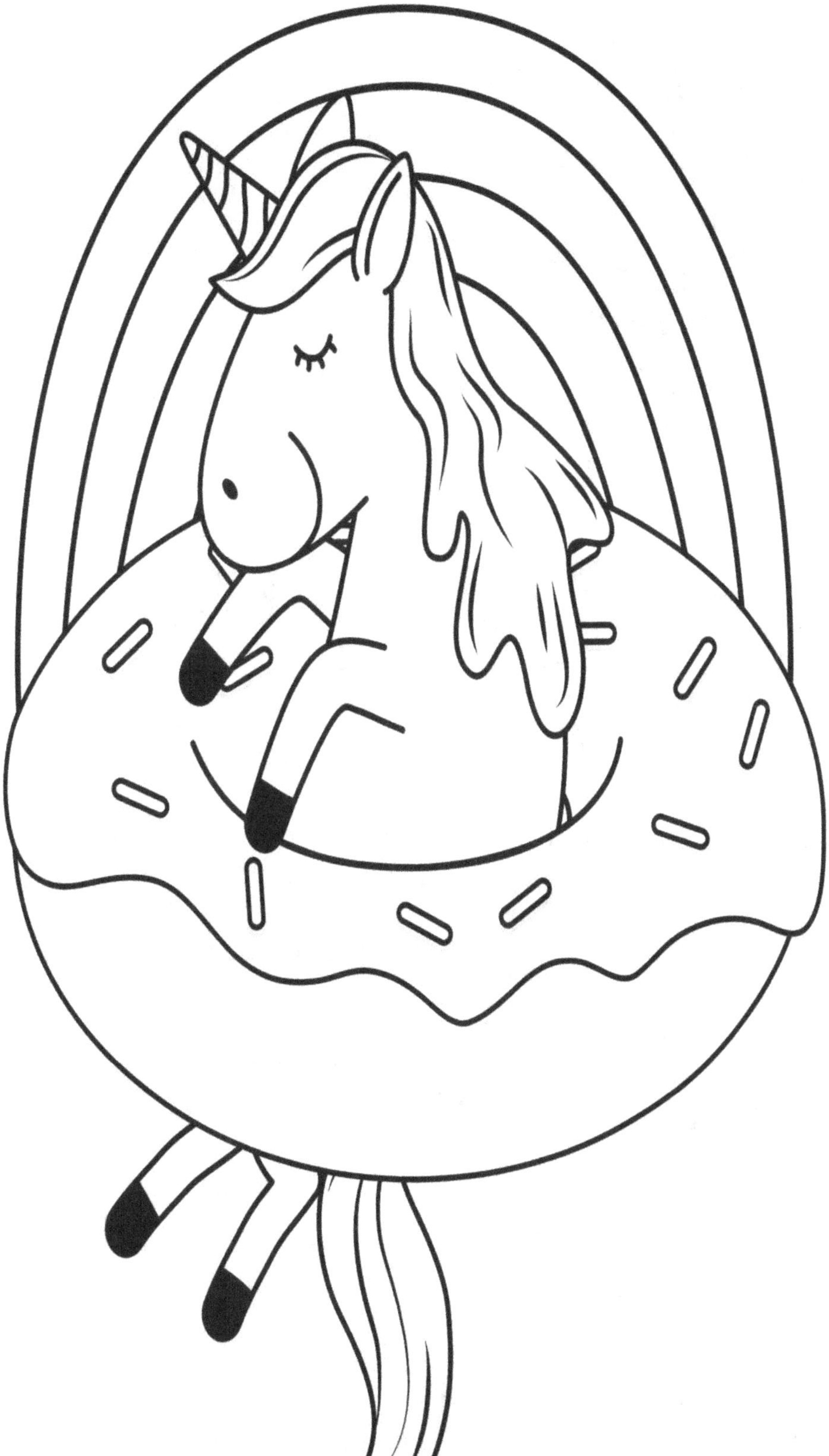

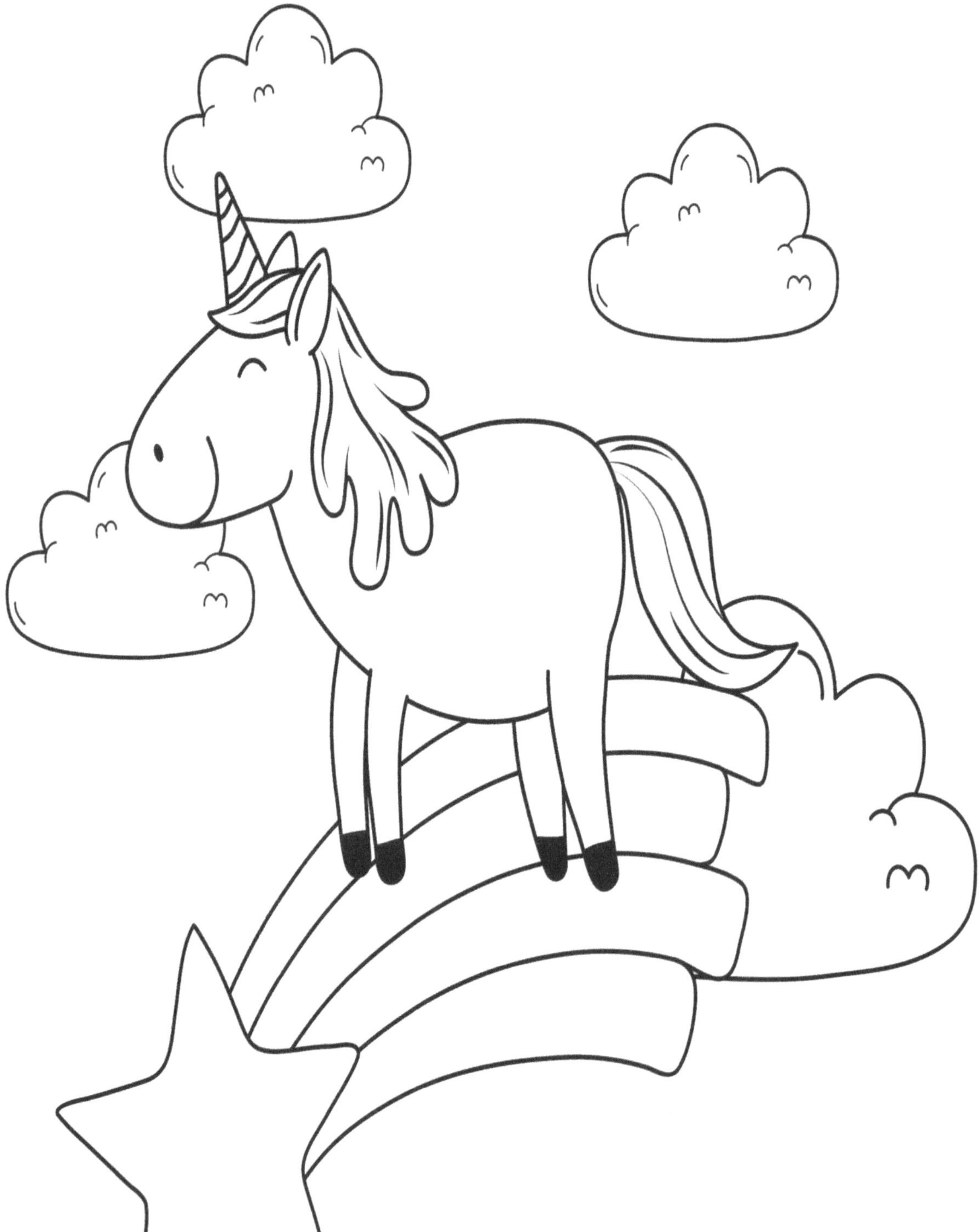

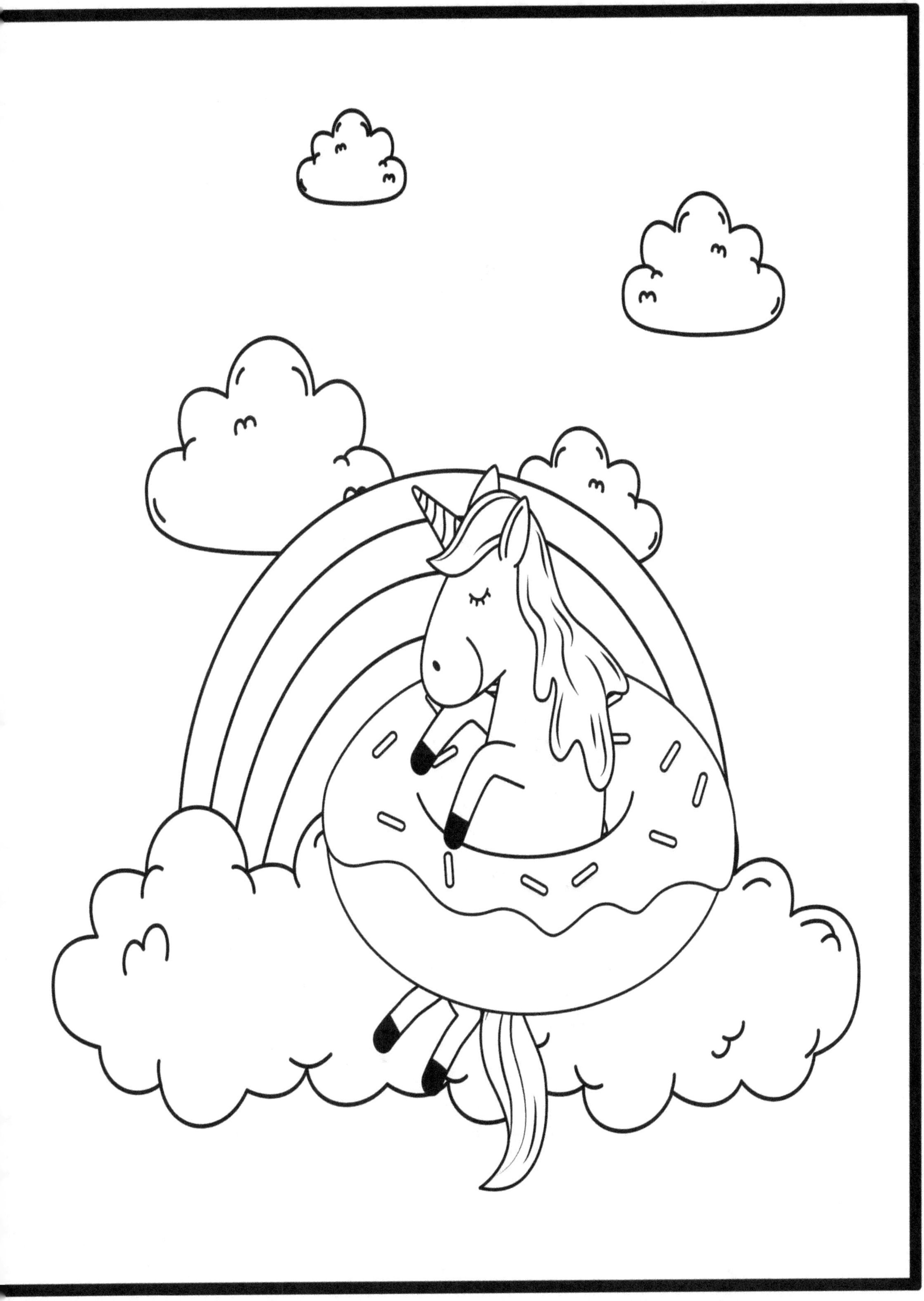

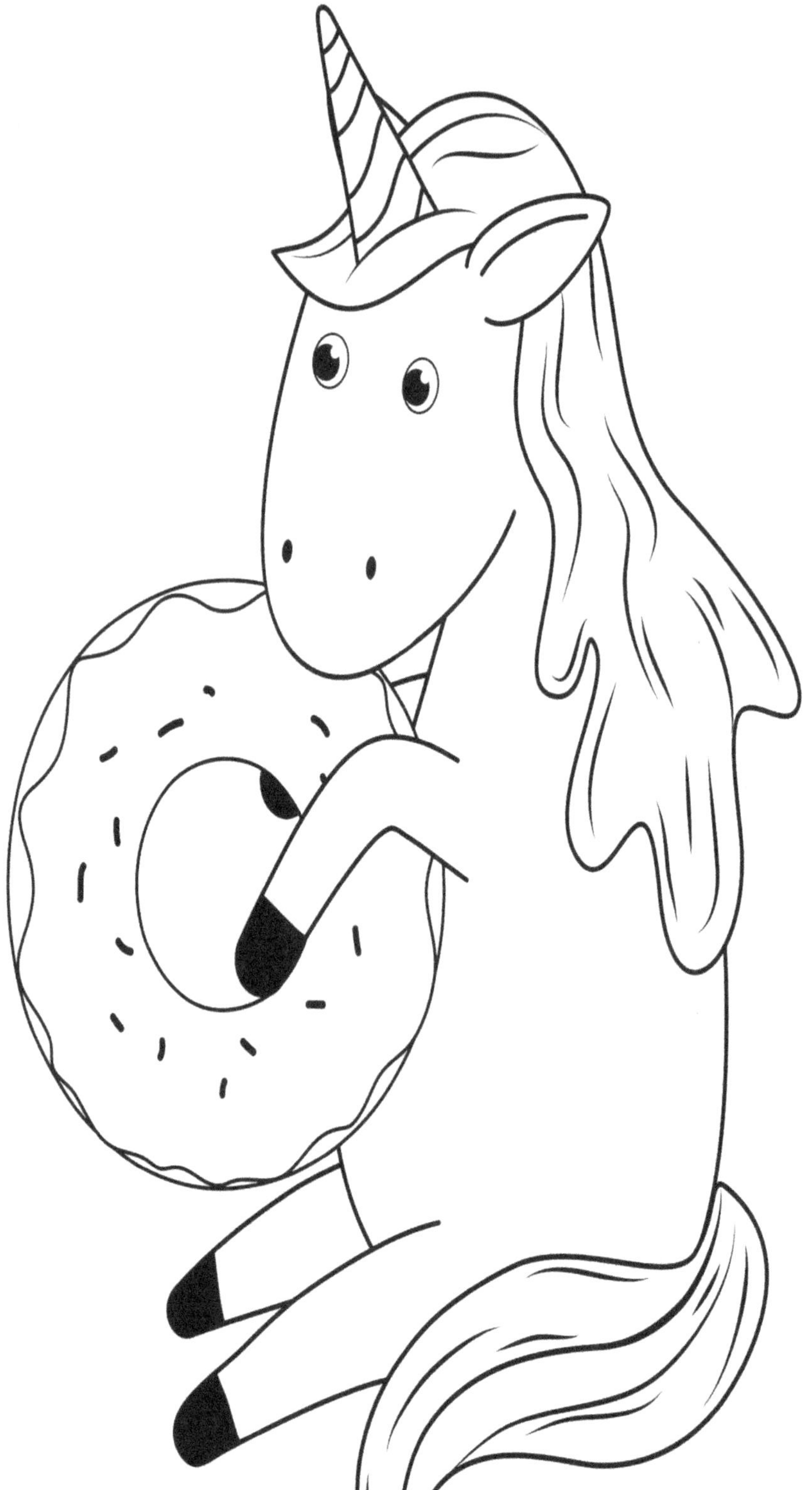

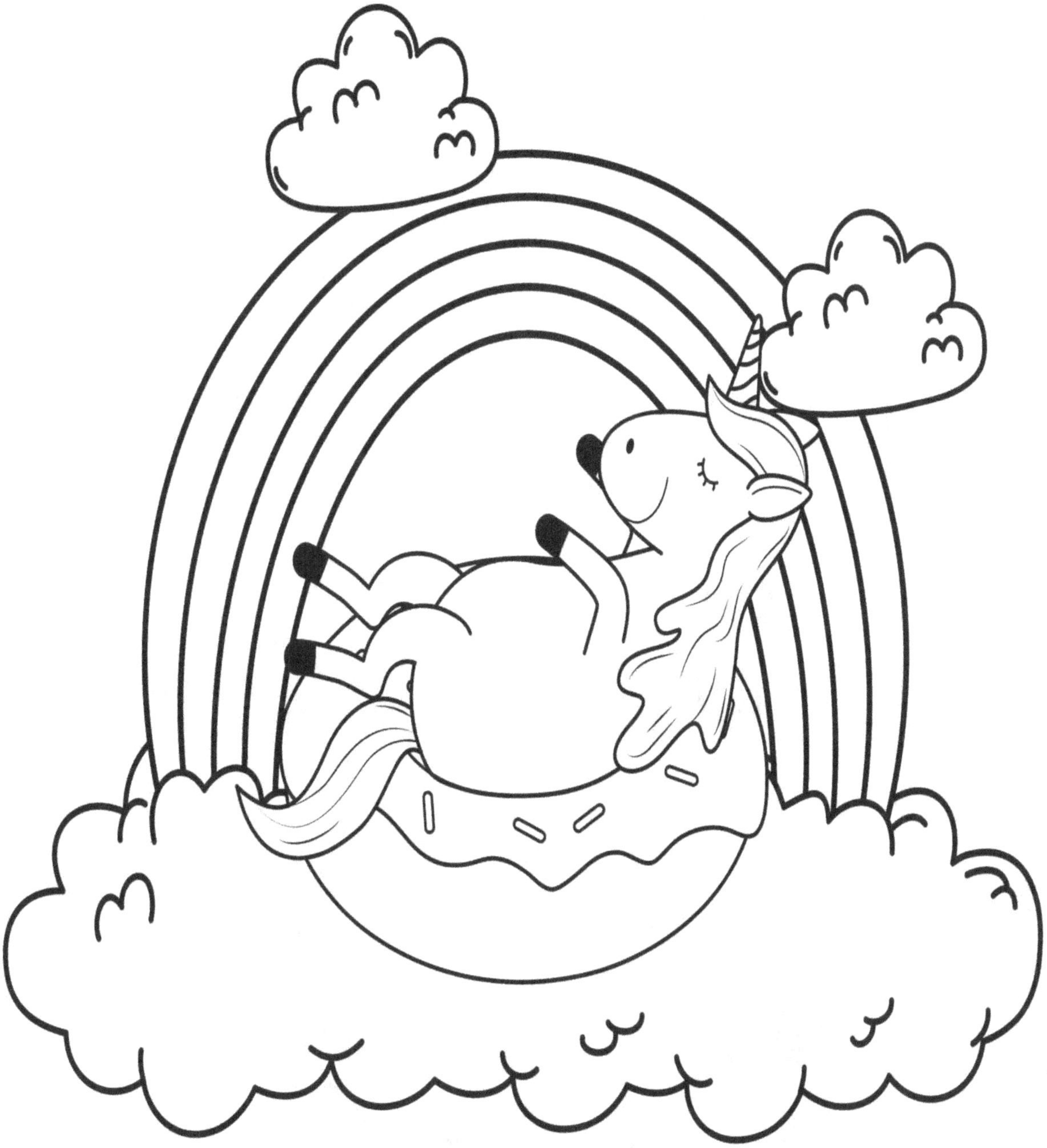

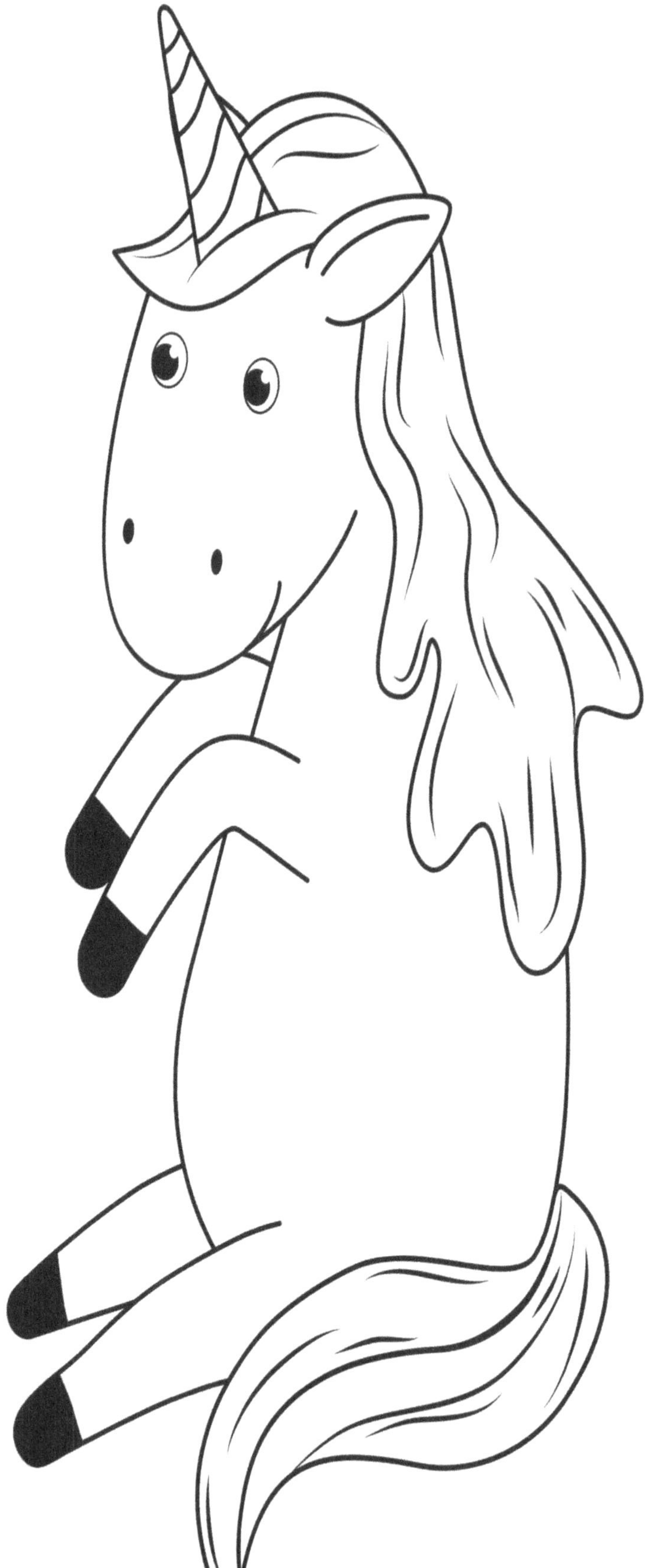

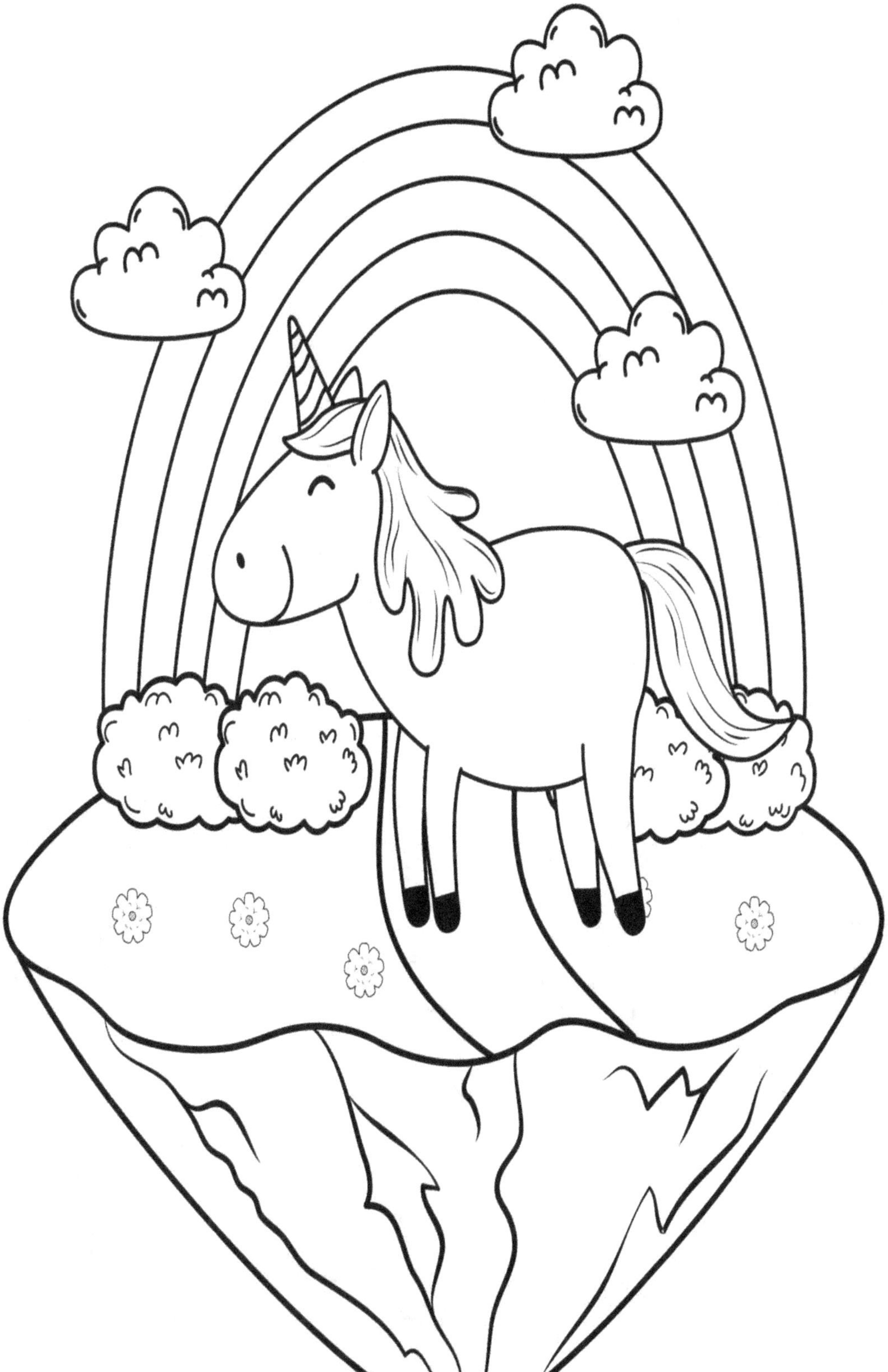

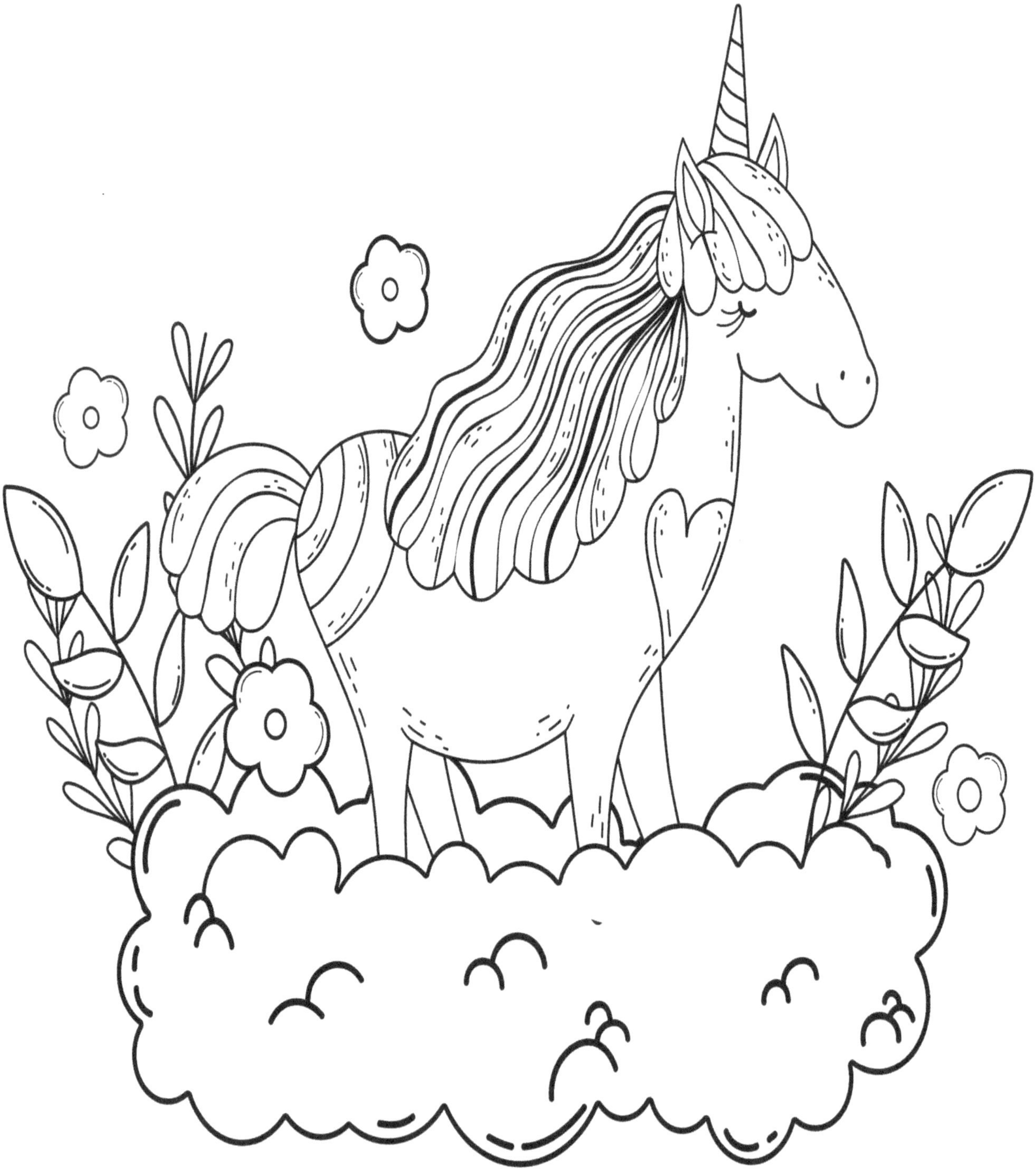

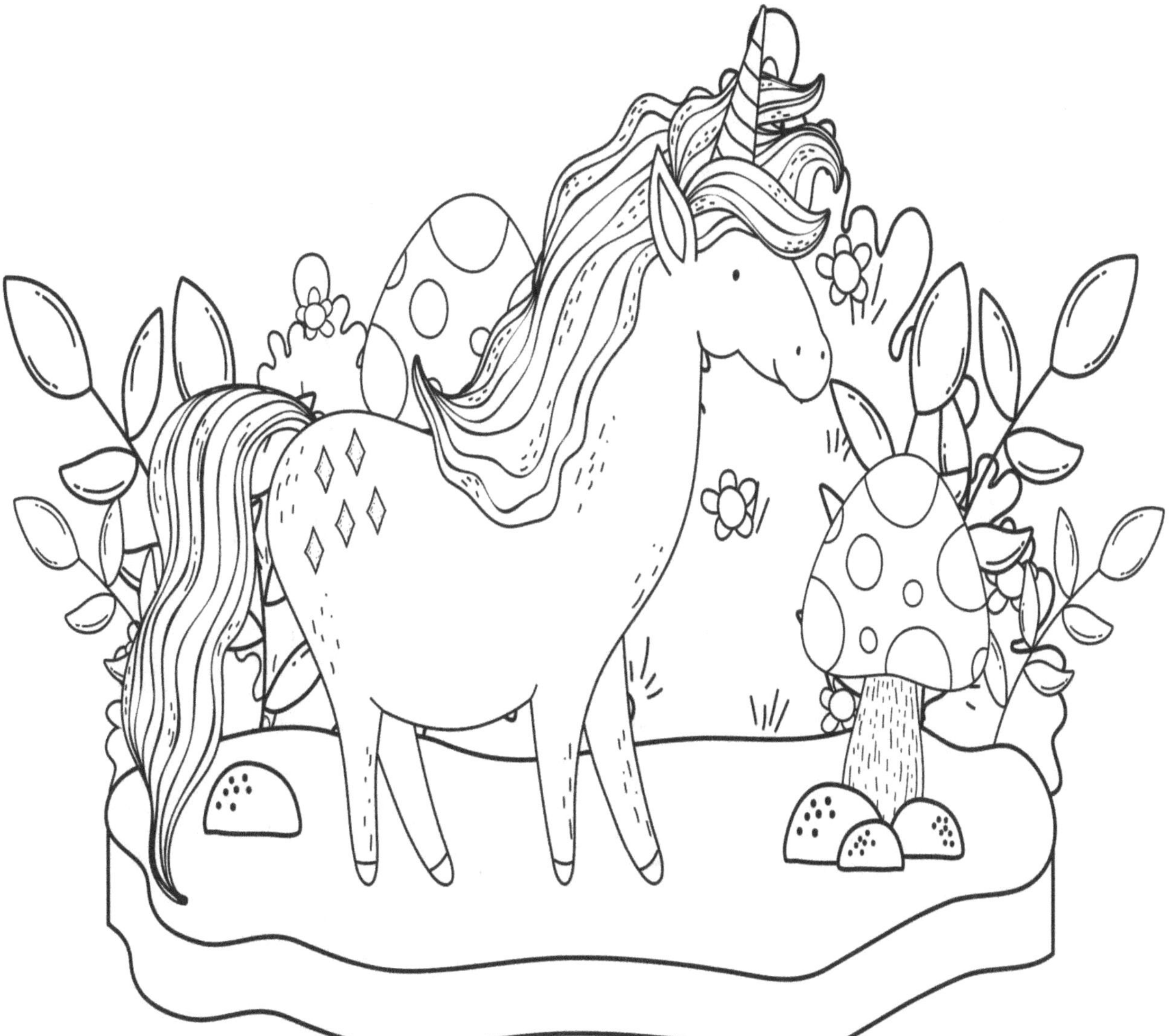

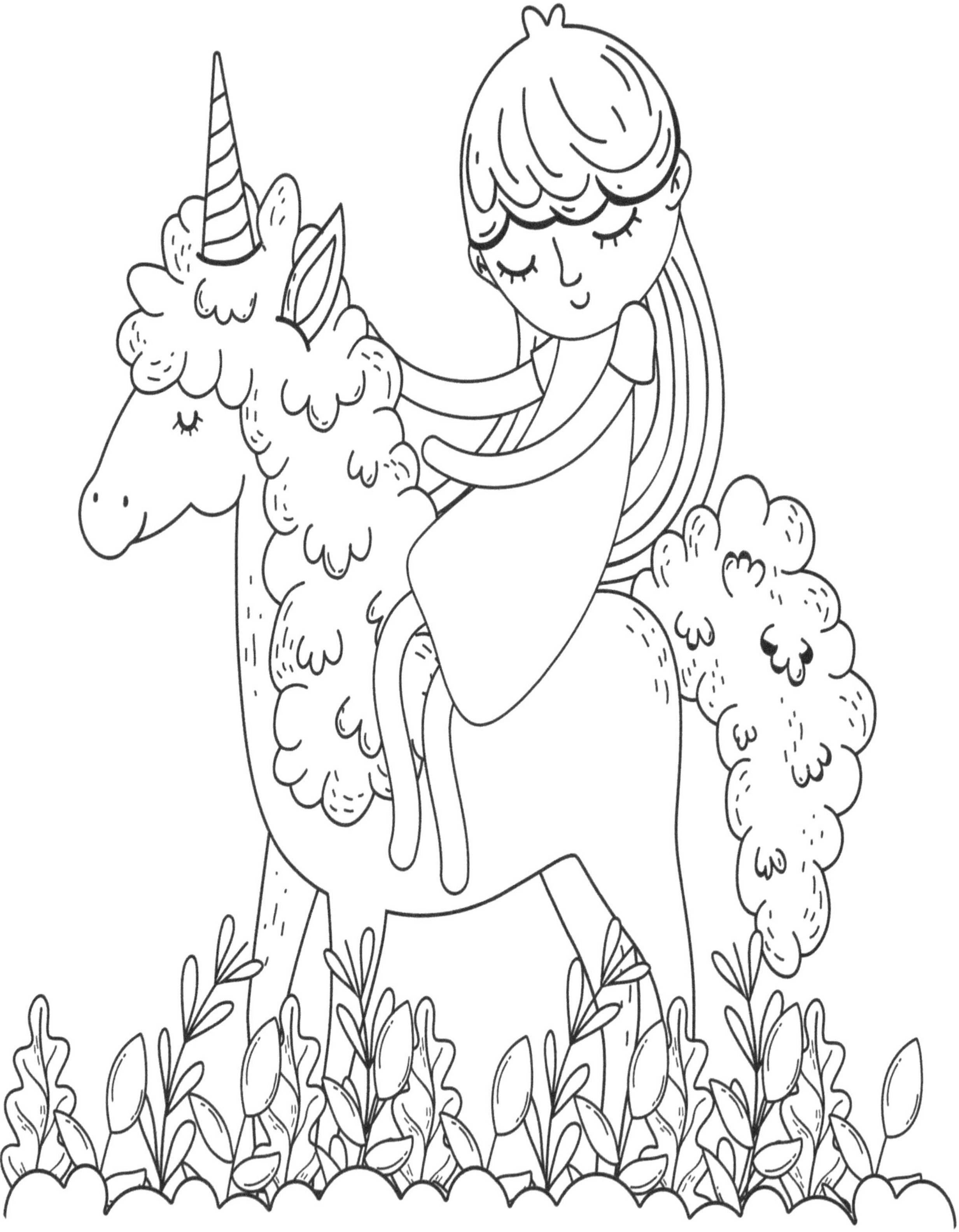

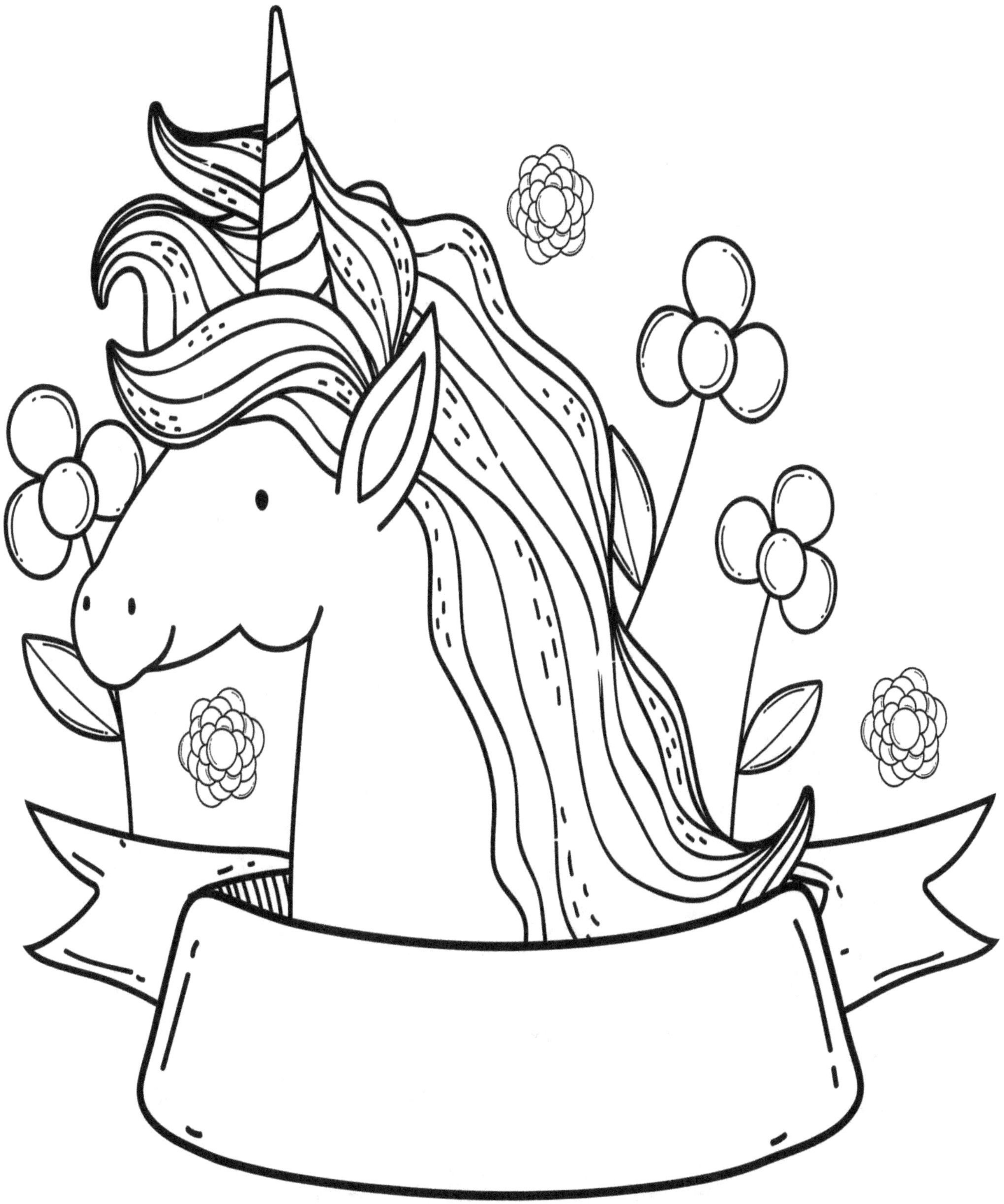

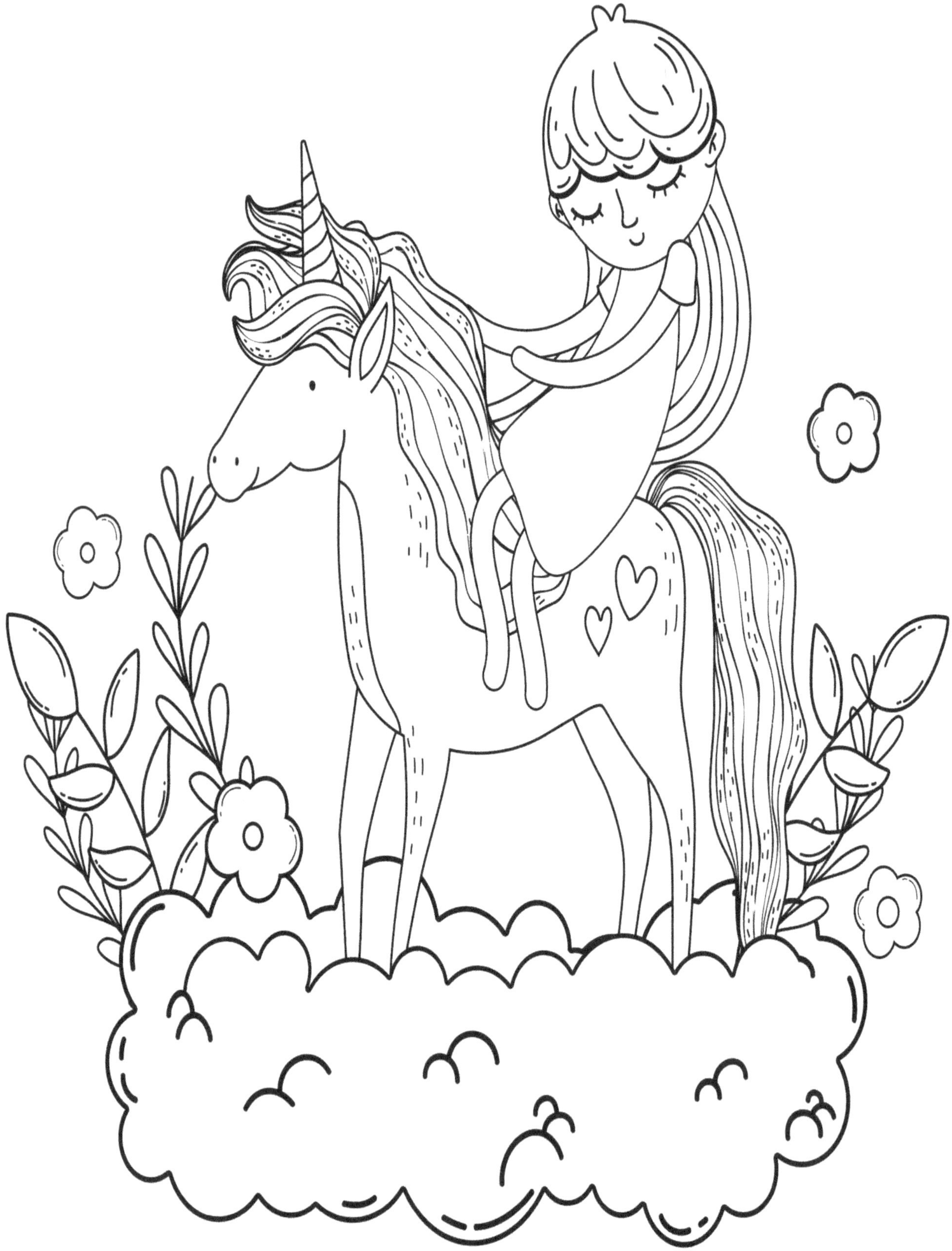

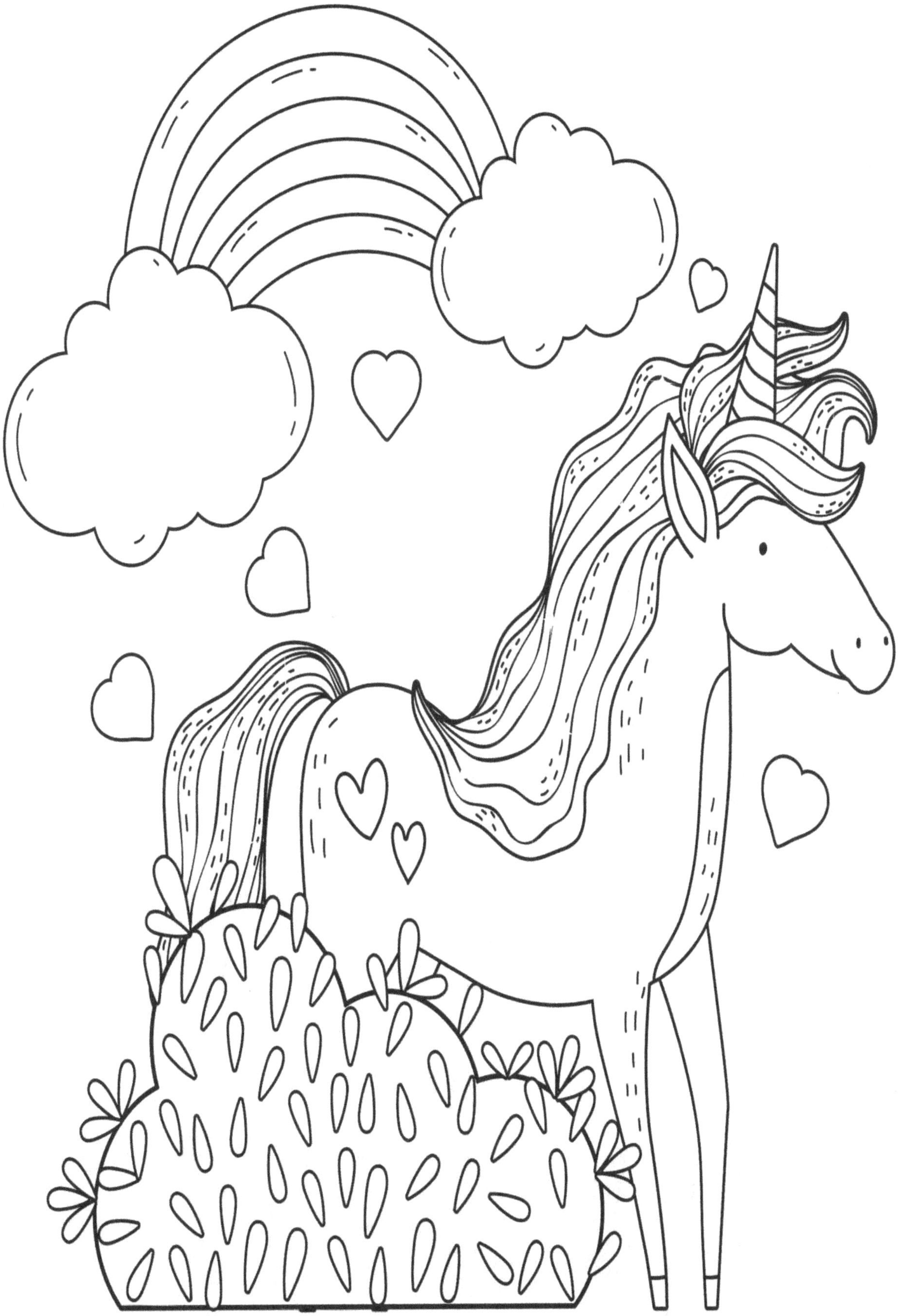

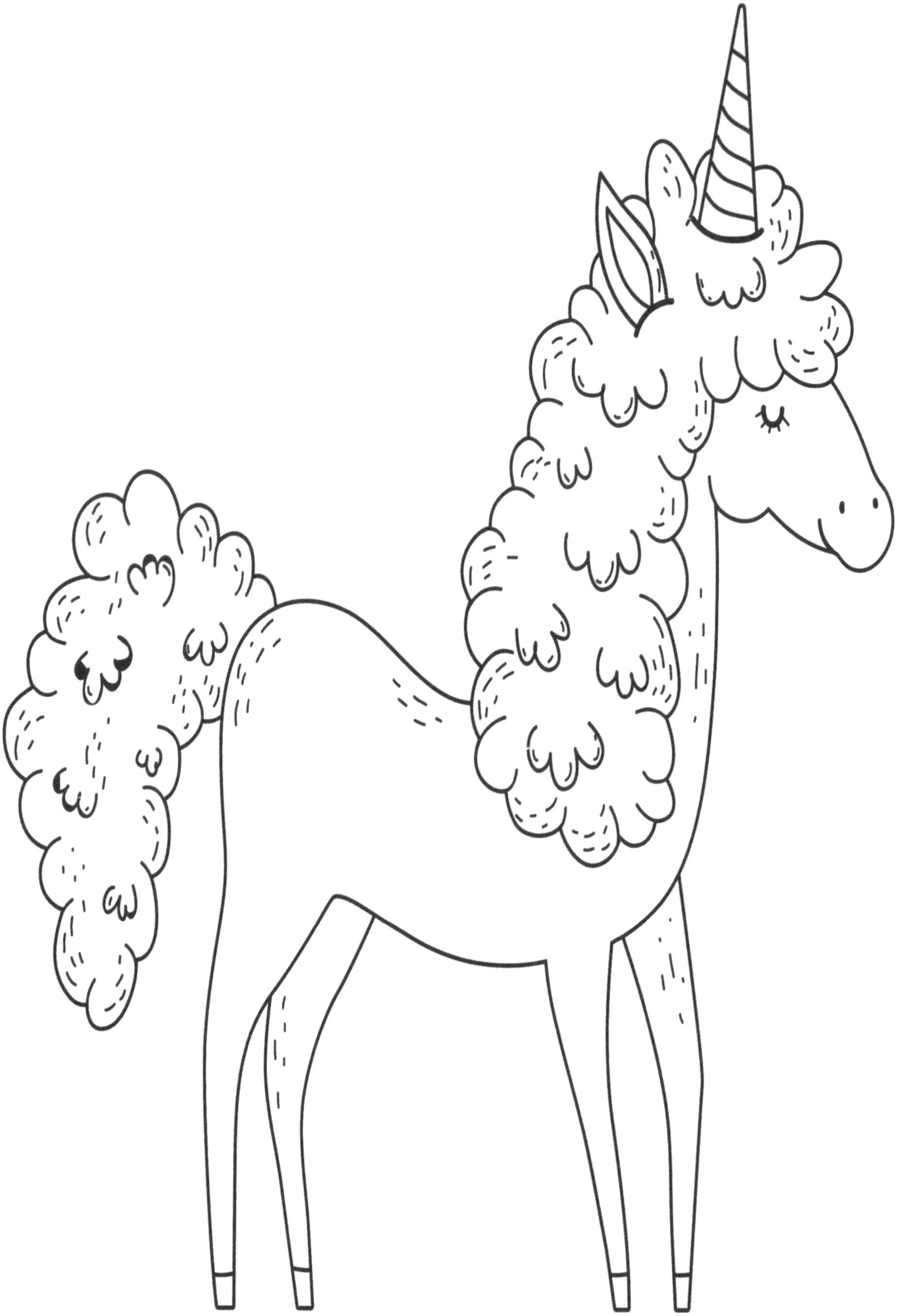

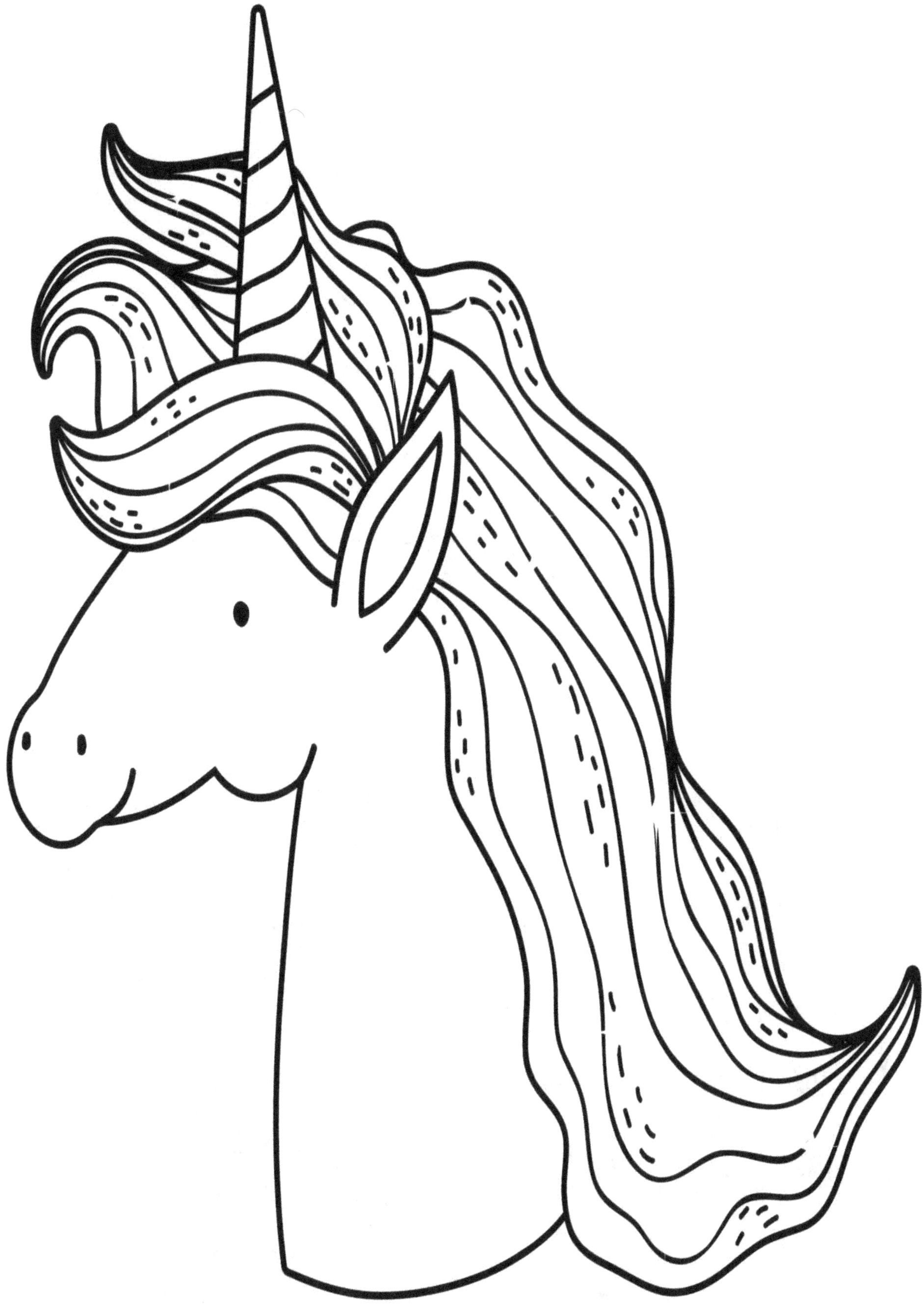

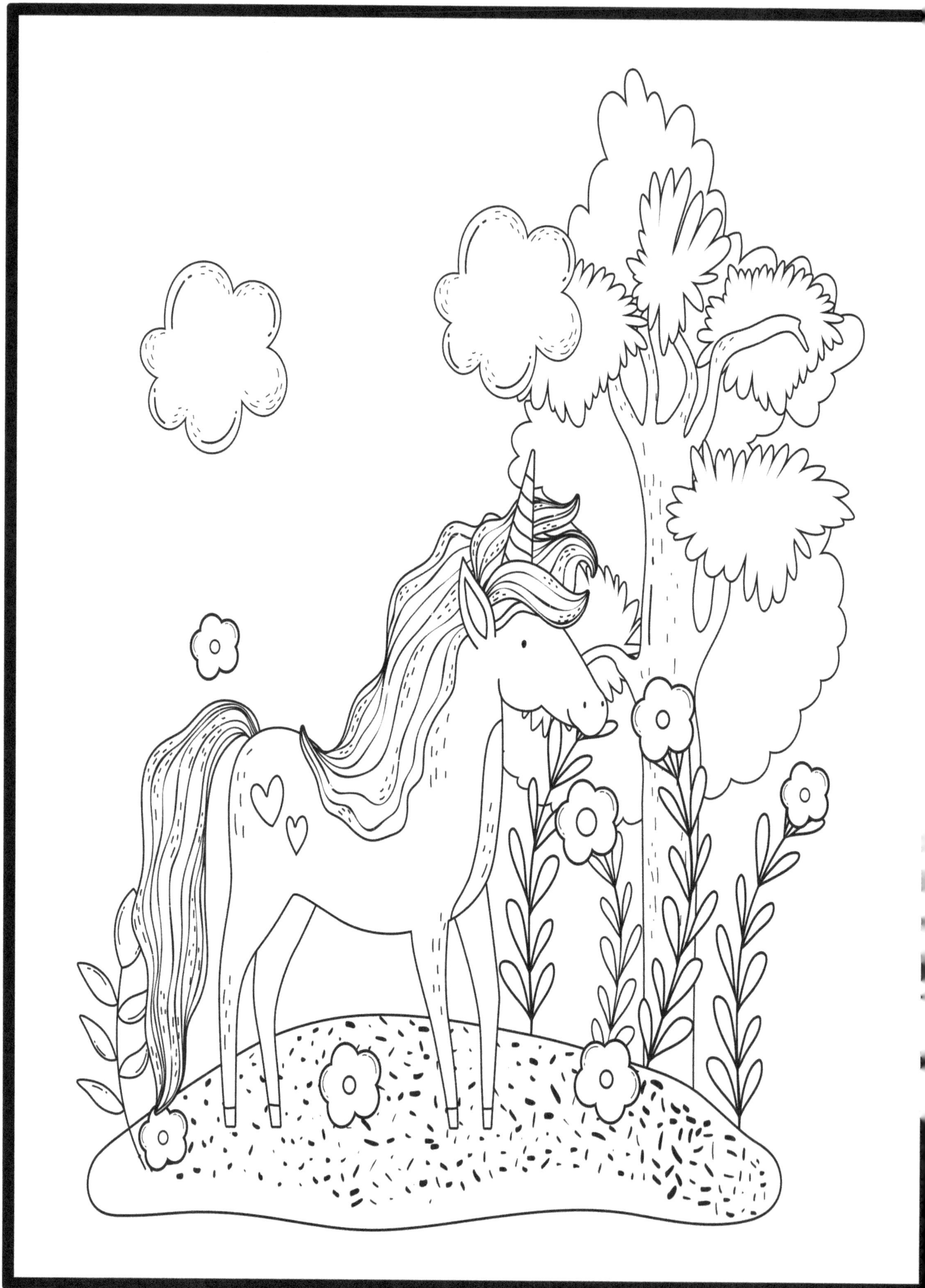

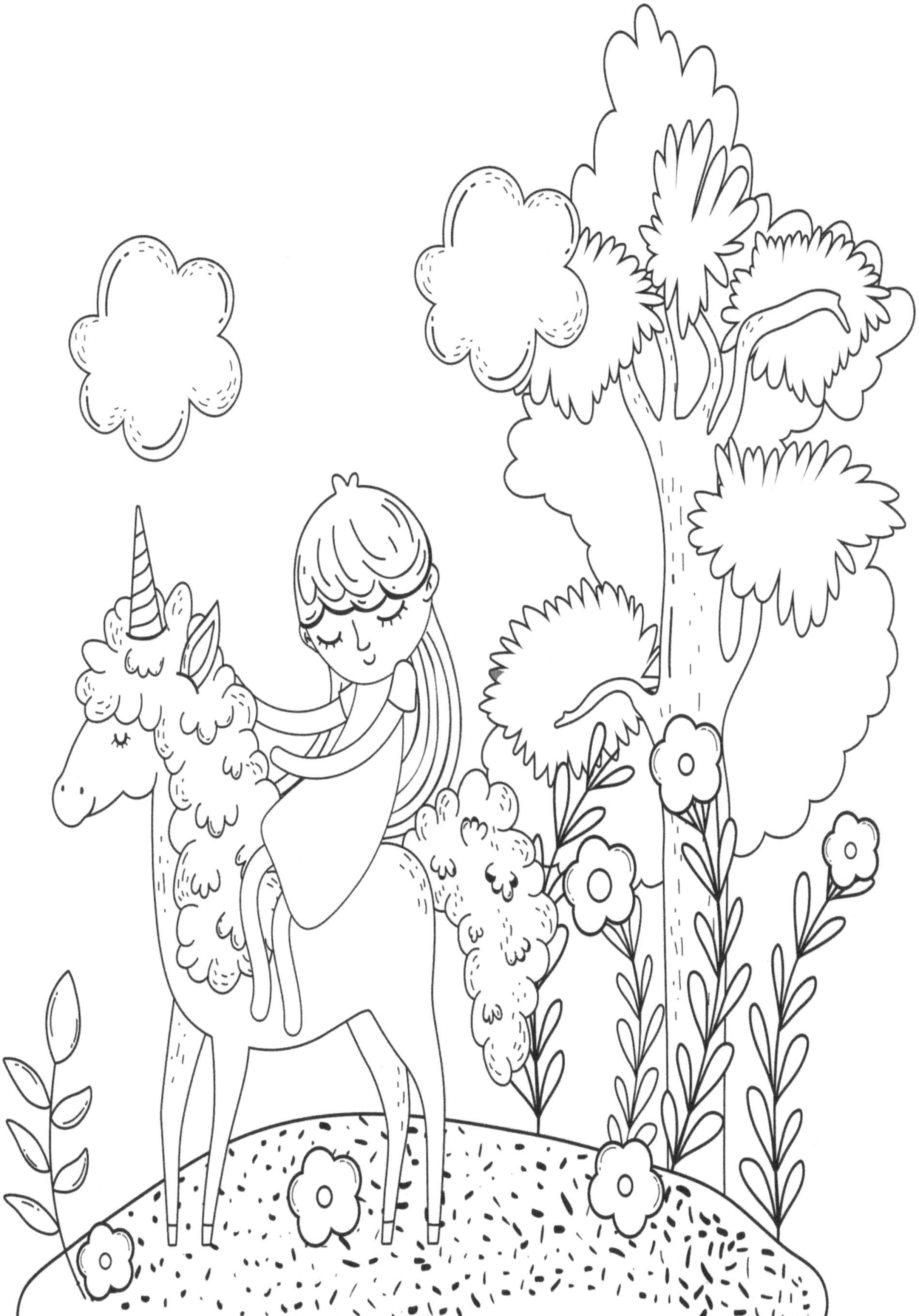

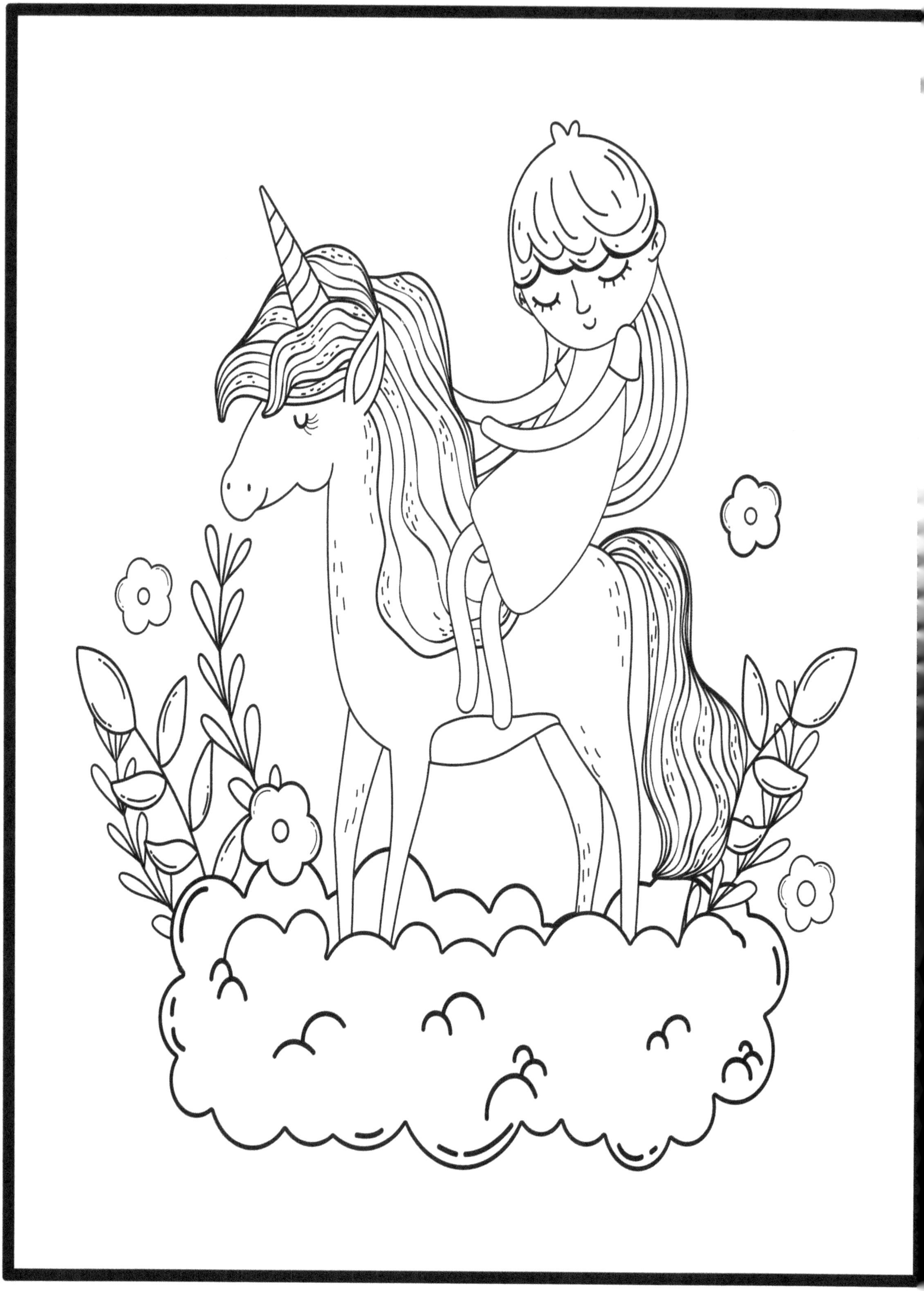

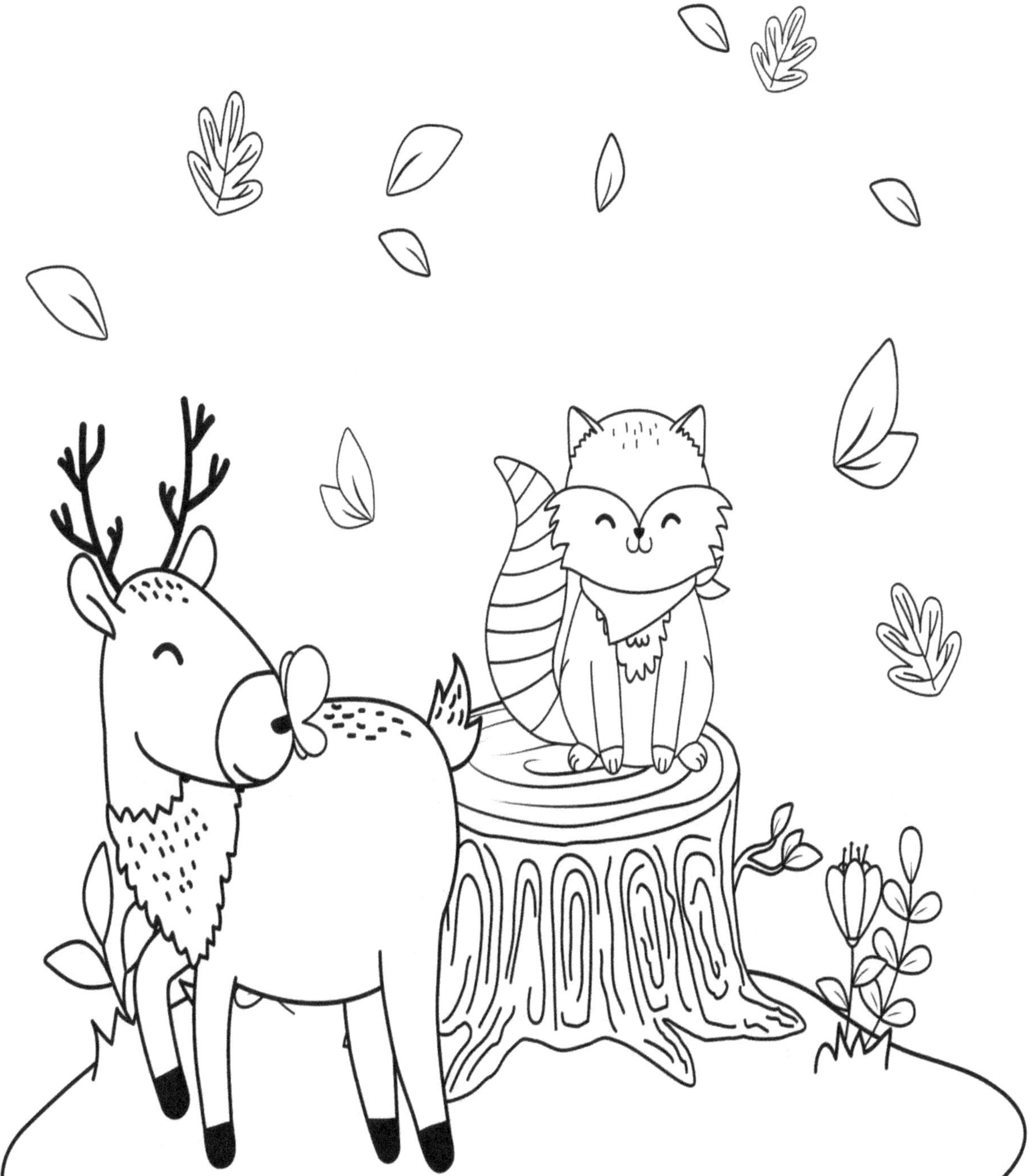

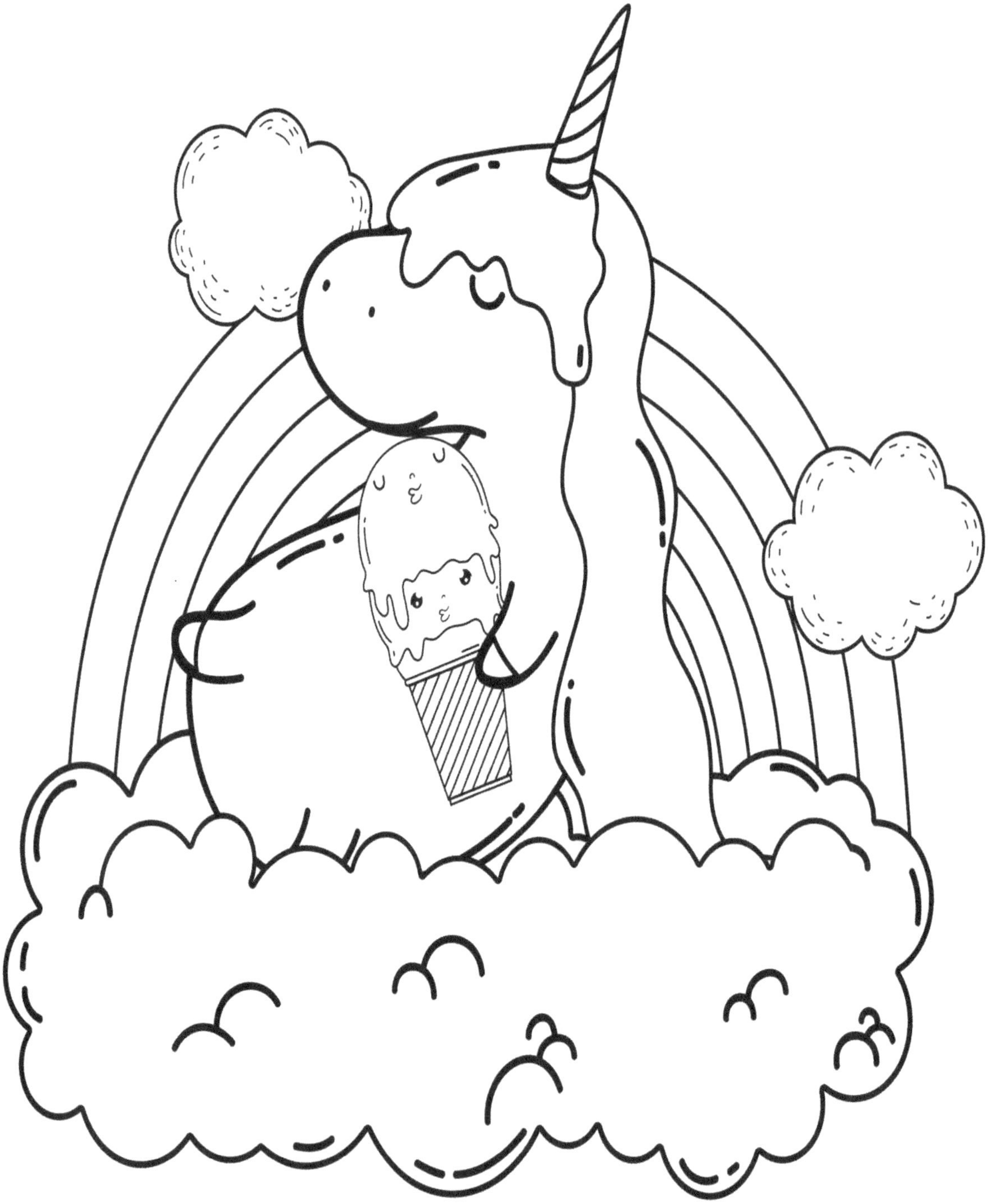

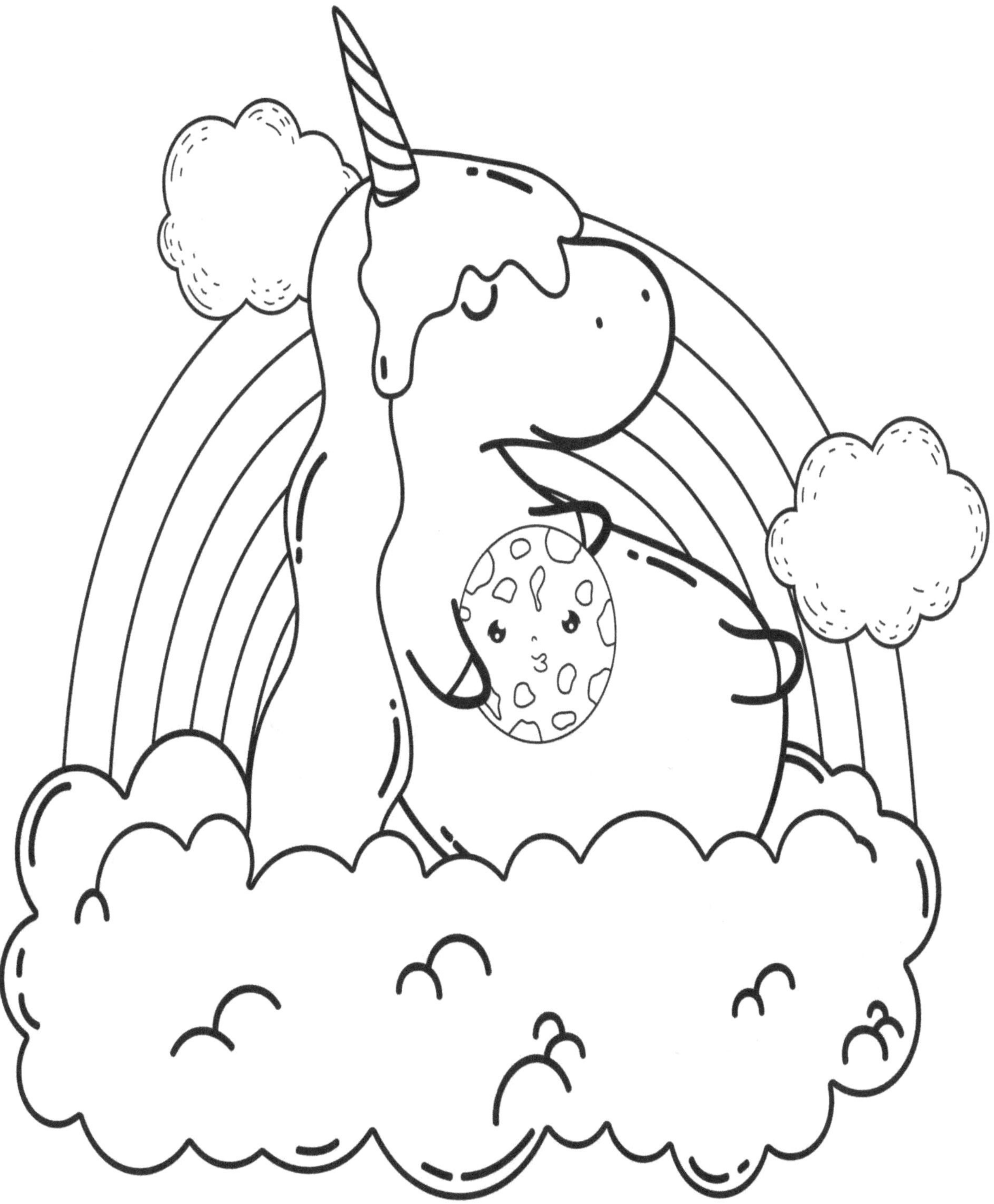

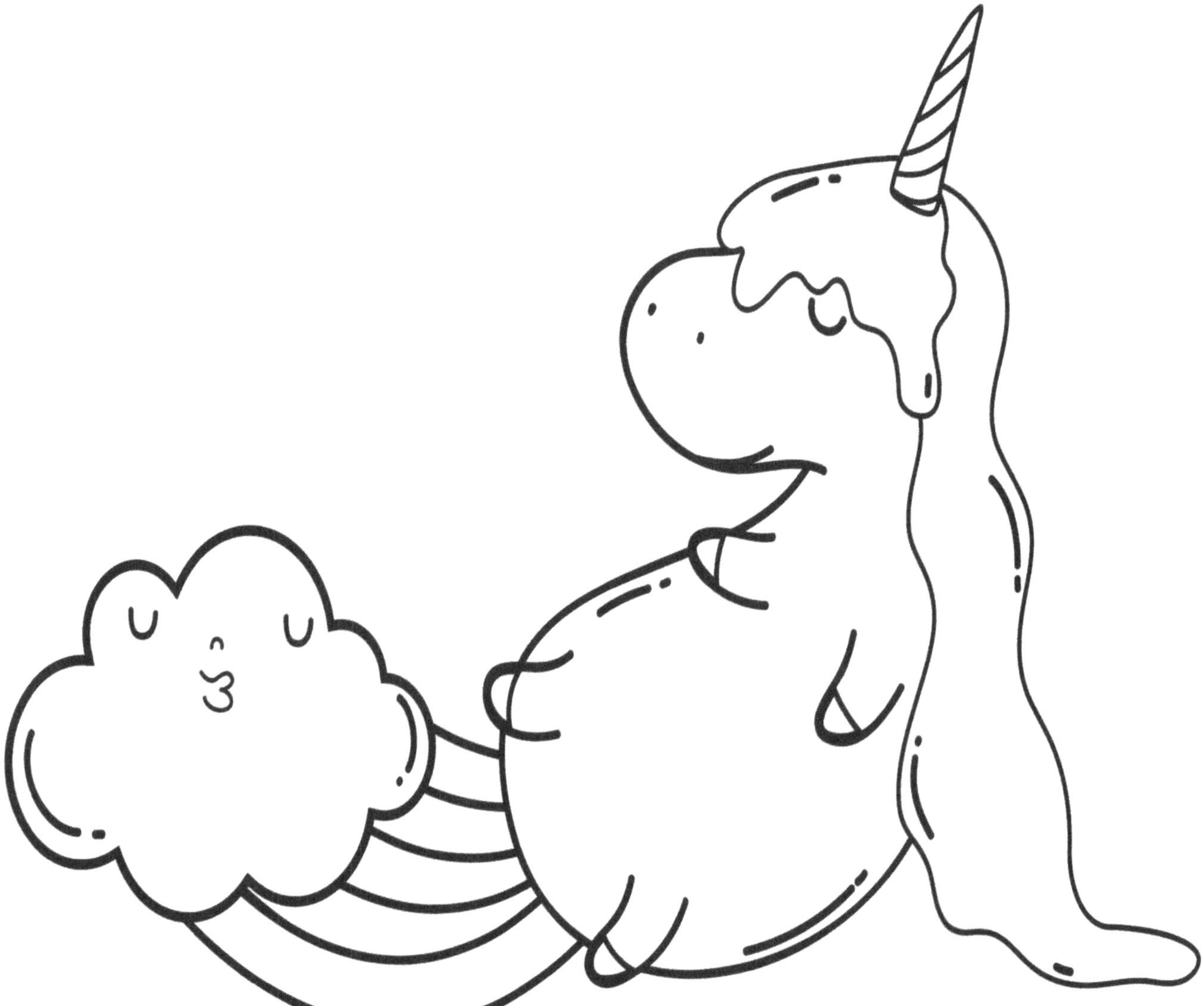

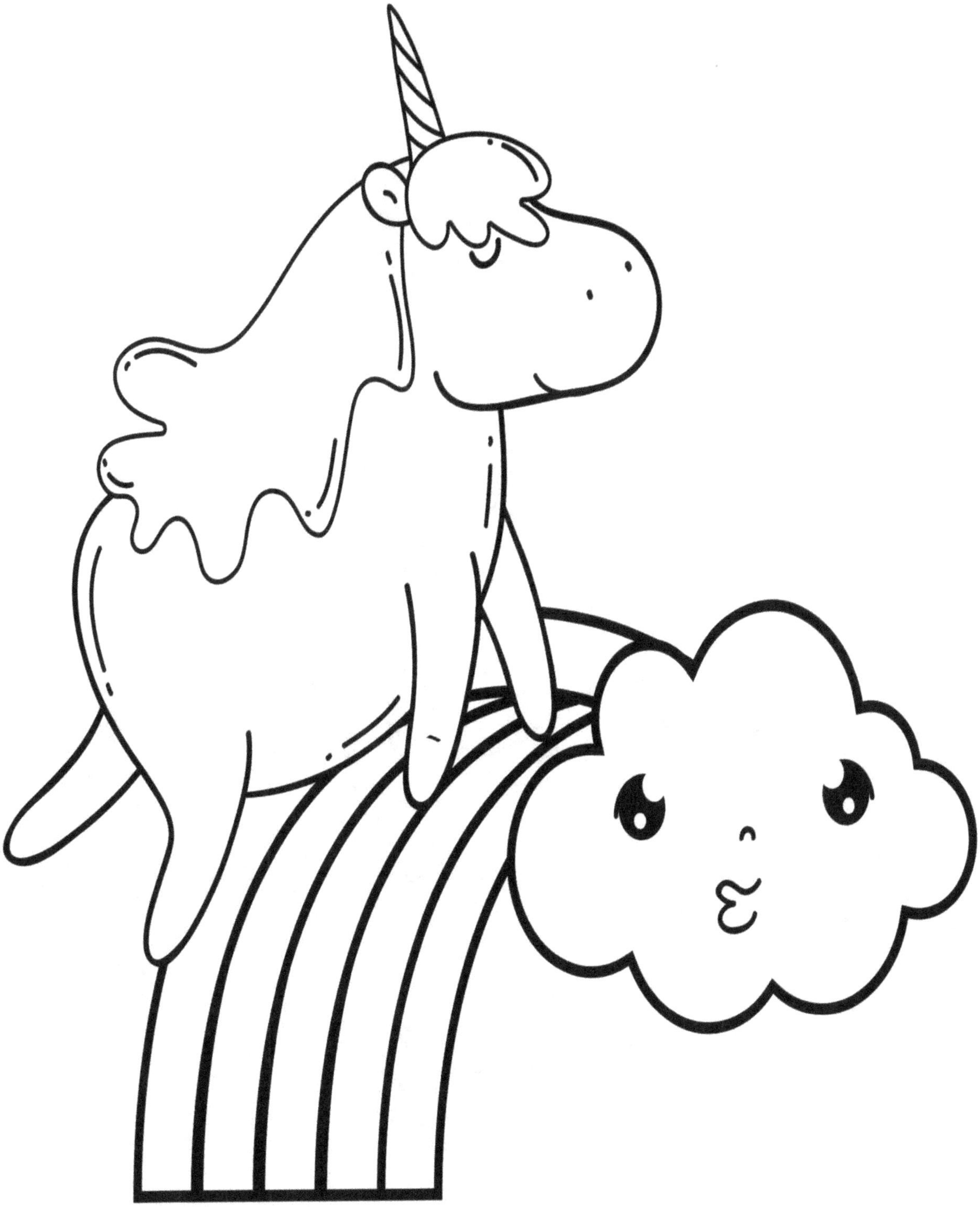

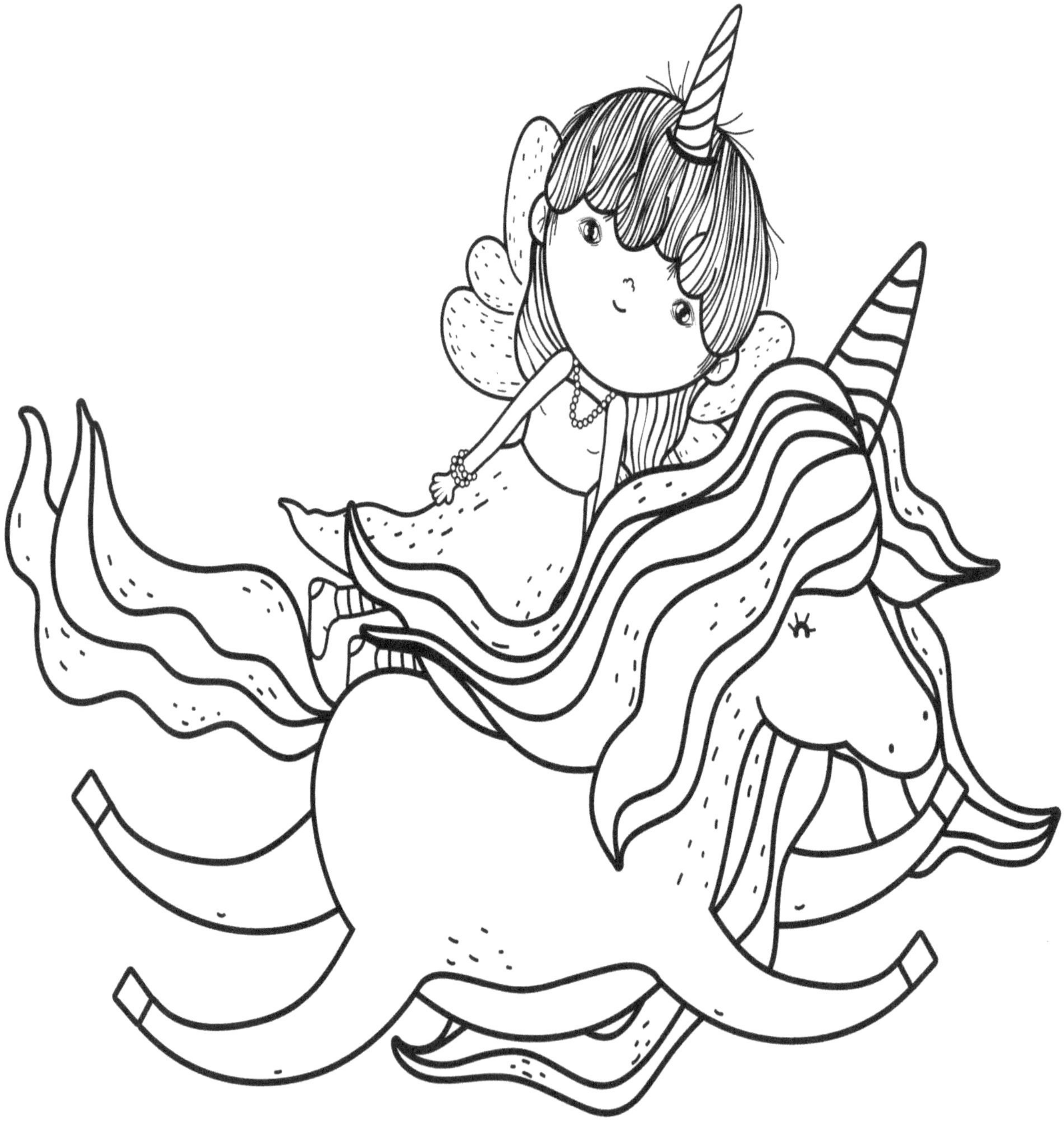

www.ingramcontent.com/pod-product-compliance
Lightning Source LLC
Chambersburg PA
CBHW080746120726
48001CB00009B/2704

* 9 7 9 8 7 2 8 8 7 9 1 2 1 *